Home To Home

The Step-By-Step Senior Housing Guide

Local Edition: Chicagoland Metro Area

To

From

Mike Fisher, Marisa Rohrer
&
Max Keller

Home To Home: The Step-By-Step Senior Housing Guide
Local Edition: Chicagoland Metro Area

ISBN: 9781734466164

© 2019 by Savior Publishing House LLC
2140 Hall Johnson Ste. 102-320
Grapevine, TX 76051
info@saviorpublishinghouse.com
817-502-9478

Mike Fisher and Marisa Rohrer
For more information, reach out to us at
www.cabinvestments.com, 708-316-0545, or
mikeandmarisa@theseniorhousingbook.com

Table of Contents

Acknowledgements

This book would not have been possible without my Mom, Sandy. She was taken from us far too soon by the devastating disease, Alzheimer's. We never had the chance to put plans like these in place for her, which has inspired and driven me to help others prepare for the future, while getting to spend as much time with their loved ones as possible.

Mike with his mom, Sandy

In 2016 I helped my parents downsize from the home that they owned for over 35 years in Illinois to move to a condo in Florida. They are currently living their best lives in Bonita Springs, FL, golfing and enjoying sunsets, and I know that there is a road map in place so that we can all enjoy life.

Marisa with her parents

Home To Home

Dedication

This book is dedicated to my late grandma, Selma Emma Keller ("Momo"), who was my best friend; Momo helped to take care of me during the first 15 years of my life, and I helped to take care of her for the last 15 years of hers.

Thank you Momo for helping me to stay in church and find my wife and for always being there for me. I am looking forward to the day when I get to see you once more in heaven.

Max Keller

Foreword

This guide has been many years in the making.

I hope that this book will serve as an instruction manual and resource for you and your family. If you found this book before there was a crisis, then congratulations! Do not wait until there is a crisis to start making a Senior Housing Plan for you or your loved one(s).

This world can sometimes be relentless.

The family that plans ahead usually has a better outcome than those that procrastinate. No one wants to think about losing their independence and then suddenly having to explore new options for the final chapter of their lives. Death and taxes are the two things that there is no escape from—it is better to plan for them.

My grandma (to whom this book is dedicated) lived a full life, well into her last years. However, no one can plan everything in life—the unexpected does happen.

When my grandfather retired in 1980 after a long career with General Motors, my grandparents still seemed to have a lot of life left to live: Grandpa was only 64 and Momo was 60.

They made plans to travel and live out their golden years in style. However, chest pains a few years later would stop that dream firmly in its tracks. Grandpa had a massive heart attack, and although he survived, he required constant care from Grandma, and their daily itinerary and choices were therefore limited.

Half a Century Later…

When Grandpa died in 1987, Grandma was alone for the first time in 47 years. However, she was very strong willed (after all, she had lived through the Great Depression) and would not be stopped. By her 90th birthday, over 20 years after Grandpa's death, she was still reading the newspaper and living alone in the same house.

Within an eight-week period, Momo went from being active to "being in a better place." As her grandson, I missed some of the signs. I think she knew that the sands of time were winding down; one thing that she did not share with us was the fact that she had been falling down and was having trouble with basic needs.

I wish I had known this—I would have moved in with her or tried to get someone to stay with her sooner. Since some of Momo's church friends had moved into a facility and then drifted off physically, mentally, or both, she was very hesitant to move into an assisted living home—she did not want to suffer the same fate.

Though she was extremely well liked and well known, we had a fairly private funeral. She outlived almost all of her friends and was one of the last to go.

Max Keller

A Simple Exercise

Can you say "Yes" to any of these questions?

- Do you have a family member with changing needs?
- Are you afraid to live by yourself but are also unwilling to give up your independence?
- Are you confused about which senior housing option is the best for you?
- Would you like to know more about what you should do with your existing house?
- Are you interested in learning more about the costs of senior housing?
- Would you like to have a solid plan in place that has many options and budgets prepared for a smooth transition (if needed)?

This book will answer these (and many more) questions. None of the options presented above are necessarily better than others—they are simply different options for different situations. In this regard, the goal of this guide is to help you understand the available options and develop your Senior Housing Roadmap as soon as possible.

This book is for senior citizen homeowners and their families. I want this book to help families that are either going through a health crisis and are overwhelmed by all the options or who are already in the planning stages regarding senior housing.

Read this guide with your family, discuss the options, and pray about them. As you and your family member(s) navigate the senior housing options available to you, I hope that the information provided herein will help shine a light on the right choices for your lives.

If you and your family want to attend a free Senior Planning Workshop, reach out to us at:

www.cabinvestments.com, 708-316-0545, or mikeandmarisa@theseniorhousingbook.com.

What This Book Will Not Do

It would be difficult to cover every option for every situation, and therefore some parts of your Senior Housing Plan will require the help of an attorney, financial planner, or other professional. It would be a disservice to you for us to claim to be all things to all people.

Our specialism is senior housing solutions— what can be done with your existing home and what are some good options for senior housing in your area. These will be the main areas of focus for this book, and we hope that you will get great value from them.

About the Publisher

Savior Publishing House LLC is a national publisher that partners with local experts in real estate who have a desire to serve their clients before themselves; in this sense, we only work with the leading experts in a given area. The local author of your book wants to serve their community and run a successful business. If you find value in this and other books, please pass them on to people you know, like, and trust. Our company's mission is to help over 1,000,000 seniors and their adult children formulate the best possible plan. Thanks to a great network of local experts, we will continue to make a difference through knowledge and education.

Disclaimer

The information in this book is not meant to replace the advice of a certified professional. Please consult a licensed advisor in matters relating to your personal and professional well-being including your mental, emotional and physical health, finances, business, legal matters, and education. The views and opinions expressed throughout the book are those of the author and do not necessarily reflect the views or opinions of any other agency, organization, employer, publisher, or company. Since we are critically-thinking human beings, the views of the author are always subject to change at any time. Any references to past performance may not be indicative of future results. No warranties or guarantees are expressed or implied by the publisher's choice to include any of the content in this volume.

If you choose to attempt any of the methods mentioned in this book, the author and publisher advise you to take full responsibility for your results. The author and publisher are not liable for any damages or negative consequences from any treatment, action, application, or preparation to any person reading or following the information in this book.

Mike Fisher, Marisa Rohrer, and Max Keller

Home To Home

Introduction

There have been many encounters with seniors over the years that have inspired us in our work, but one in particular will always resonate with me: During my time in the building and remodeling trade, I was building an addition to my friend's home that would enable his parents to move in with him and his family. My friend's father, Jim, was living with Parkinson's disease and didn't want to give up his home or his independence and this provided the perfect compromise. One day, Jim said to me, "Getting old is not for sissies". I will always remember his words—seniors have so many challenges to overcome, at a time when they should be enjoying their lives and loved ones.

In everything we do, both in our professional lives and our personal lives, we strive to live by our three core values: Live fully, love openly, and make a difference.

My journey into real estate began when I was in the building and remodeling trade—I could feel the toll the abuse and wear-and-tear of the work was having on my body. I was self-employed and didn't have a retirement plan—I knew I needed to come up with a plan for my future. In 2003, I made the decision to buy one house a year. By 2016, I had accumulated 28 properties that were all providing a steady cash flow, had started a property management company, and had begun buying distressed properties to refurbish and sell to investors from all over the world. Currently, I own and manage a large portfolio of properties and now educate aspiring real estate investors on strategies to maximize their cash flow. Marisa and I are also partnering with the Continuity of Care Association to assist seniors making the transition into senior living facilities.

Driven by our values and our desire to make a difference to the lives we touch, we believe in adding value to the experience our clients have with us. We believe we add value, not only in the services we provide, but also by referring our clients to a wealth of qualified professionals.

In our professional and personal experiences, we have seen many families struggling with finding the right direction to take when looking to help their seniors make a transition. We immediately identified a need to use our knowledge and expertise to help our friends, family, and community—helping to make their lives easier, and lift some of the burden transition brings. We often hear that the days are long, but the years are short. Our time on Earth is valuable and all to short and the time we do have should be spent enjoying our lives and loved ones.

We are able to offer our clients an opportunity to utilize the concierge program which will pay the upfront costs for helping to get their home ready to sell at no additional cost. Our sellers can borrow money for home updates, storage, moving, painting, cleaning... and pay back the money at the sale of the home. No fees, no interest!

We are also able to offer our clients a quick, as-is cash sale if that is what fits their needs. Let us use our network to help you find the best path for you!

Home To Home

Chapter 1: Your Current Situation

Our companies have helped hundreds of people with their home situation, and the formula for dealing with a housing change is very simple: the more you plan ahead, the better the outcome will be.

Planning ahead is the key, but how do you start?

Dave Ramsey, the famous financial planner, recommends that his listeners should obtain long-term care insurance at the age of 60. We will discuss long-term care insurance later. However, I recommend that you start your Senior Housing Plan—for you or your loved one—at or before the age of 60.

According to the Centers for Disease Control and Prevention, life expectancy is currently 78.8 years.[1]

In this regard, putting a plan in place 18 years early can smooth out some of the speed bumps that life and Murphy's Law may put in our way.

---

[1] Source: National Center for Health Statistics," *Centers for Disease Control and Prevention*, 3 May 2017. Retrieved from www.cdc.gov/nchs/fastats/life-expectancy.html

Chapter 2: Your Ideal Destination

It is important to map out exactly where you or your senior want to be as you transition into senior housing since your ideal destination has a great deal to do with the type of lifestyle you envision having.

A Tale of Two Roadmaps

Option One – Normal Pace

Perhaps everything is going well now and you are in the planning phase. Maybe you picked this book up early and decided that this roadmap is too important to leave to chance. During this planning stage, you will figure out what your goals, dreams, and desires are. It is time to start figuring out exactly what sort of housing is the right fit and run through some "what if" scenarios in order to test your plan.

For example:

- If your spouse dies, where do you want to live?

- If you get sick or fall down and injure yourself, are you going to move in with a family member or continue living by yourself?

The ideal situation refers to, everything going well, what you would like to see happen. So, if something were to happen, such as a sickness requiring extra medical care, what would the ideal outcome be for you? These are the types of conversations that you want to have with your family right now.

If you are the child of a senior, read this book with your parent and say, "Mom/Dad, if you were to need extra care, would you want to live with us? We would love to have you living with us. You would not be a burden, and we would take care of you. We love you!"

Alternatively, you could say the opposite: "Mom/Dad, we love you, but we are not equipped to take care of you. If x, y, or z happens, where would you want to live?"

There are no right or wrong answers.

You are not a good or bad person based on these conversations—let God do the judging! These are the types of conversations that you want to have now, ahead of time.

Another great question could be, "Mom/Dad, if you needed some extra care, where would you want to live? Would you want to live close to church? Would you want to be close to us?"

Max comes from a big family, and they all live in the same general area. However, when his grandmother died, her extended family were not close, both emotionally and geographically.

If your senior needs new housing options, would they stay in their own city or state, where they have their local network, or would they move across town, state, or even country to be somewhere closer to their adult children?

These are definitely questions that you want to get worked out ahead of time. In this regard, simply assuming that somebody wants to move or stay is not the way to go. Talk about this ahead of time and see what the ideal destination and situation would be if extra care was needed.

Option Two – Fast-Track Pace

Something has happened, and you need to make a senior housing switch immediately. You did not plan for something major to happen or the need for drastic change.

What do you do now?

Maybe you ordered this book or got it from a friend or pastor and you are trying to figure out what to do next. Our goal is to make this difficult time easier for you. You can read this book from start to finish, but if you need to fast forward to the information you need right now, you certainly can.

Use the checklists in each chapter to assist you in building your roadmap. For more information, reach out to us at:

www.cabinvestments.com, 708-316-0545, or mikeandmarisa@theseniorhousingbook.com.

Remember that although something may have happened necessitating a change in your senior's housing situation—and although there may not have been a plan in place to navigate through it—there is a more ideal destination available.

You may not be able to put a perfect plan together in a short time, but we are confident that if you use the information in these chapters, you can still put an excellent plan together. An ideal plan depends on your family and what is important to you.

Planning Checklist

If you and an adult child are working together to make these decisions, the checklist below will need to be answered by each person and then combined in order to figure out the ideal situation.

Fast-Track Checklist

- ❏ Should you sell the house or keep it?
- ❏ What type of care is necessary based on the medical facts?
- ❏ What type of facility do you want to be in?
- ❏ What kinds of amenities are important to you?
- ❏ What geographical location do you want to stay in?
- ❏ What is your monthly budget?

❏ How long will the resources last?

❏ What are your current mobility needs, and how will that affect the choice of where to live next?

❏ What type of care is needed and what facilities offer them?

Building the Roadmap

After each major chapter, there will be a checklist in abbreviated form for you to review.

For more information, reach out to us at:

www.cabinvestments.com, 708-316-0545, or mikeandmarisa@theseniorhousingbook.com.

Chapter 3: Selling Your Home

"I need to sell my house quickly! Can you come over today?" This was an urgent request on a normal Tuesday morning to a real estate agent's office. What could have happened that would have caused someone who had lived in their house for over 40 years to call someone they had never met and ask them to sell their home in 20 minutes?

This customer needed to sell her house quickly because she had waited too long to ask for help. As the agent went over her options, she became adamant about selling that day: "I need to sell the home before I lose it. I have not been making the payments, and it is going to auction next week."

The agent thought, "I wish she had called me for help six months ago. The outcome would have been much better."

The house was in rough shape, and her kids and relatives were not helping. Fortunately, the agent was able to arrange the purchase of her home before it went to auction; in addition, the customer was able to keep some equity for her retirement and is currently living with family members.

What Has Been Happening Lately?

Change in Health

There can be many reasons why someone may decide to sell their home, but the one that we run into most often is a change in health. When someone no longer has the mobility or confidence to live at home, they often sell the house and move out. If that person does not have a support network in place or people who can move in with them, it is wiser to sell.

Your change in health can be sudden. One day you can be active, driving your own car, and doing whatever you want, and the next you can be in the hospital recovering from emergency surgery—some events are difficult to predict.

For this reason, we encourage you to plan and do as much as you can ahead of time. Planning for worst-case scenarios sounds strange, but if disaster strikes, you and your family will be better prepared.

Death of a Loved One

Another recent event could be the death of a husband or wife. Max's grandfather passed away in 1987; however, his grandmother continued to live in the same home that she had shared with him for over 20 years afterwards. Although his death was traumatic for her, his grandmother wanted to stay in her home.

For some, the idea of living in the house in which their spouse had passed away is too much of an emotional burden—the mementos, pictures on the wall, and memories are just too much to handle. In such a situation, a change of location can sometimes help the healing process.

How Much Time Will You Have to Make Your Decision?

The timing for when you and your family make a decision really depends on the situation and recent events. Quick changes in your health and well-being may require quicker decisions. If everyone involved is healthy and feeling great and you are simply evaluating what may happen down the road, you obviously do not need to make these decisions quickly.

What are the options available for your (or your parents') current house? It really depends on how much time you have and the house's condition.

However, do not hesitate for too long. Every day in the news, there is someone famous and well off who either had a major health challenge or passed away suddenly without a proper plan in place. Since there was no Senior Housing Plan, everyone involved was not prepared for the sudden changes that resulted from the event.

Do not let this happen to you. Start today!

Whether you are in action mode today or in long-term preparation mode, do not wait until something happens to start planning. Dave Ramsey talks about financial planning and saving for things that we know are going to happen in the future.

If and when your family faces a health challenge, dealing with it alone is going to be difficult enough. By putting your plan in place, you can fully focus on the health challenge and not have to worry so much about your housing options—that part of the plan will already be place, ready to be implemented.

Benefits of a Plan

The benefits of creating your Senior Housing Roadmap early are significant. If you plan the sale of your home ahead of time, you can usually get more money for your house, which means more choices as far as your senior housing location is concerned.

Great senior housing facilities can have long waiting lists, and when there is an opening, you have to move quickly. You do not want to find out that your name is next on the waiting list and you only have a few weeks to begin planning the sale of your home.

If you have already spoken with housing professionals, you will be in a great position for a smooth transition—less stress and better outcomes are the goal. If you do not plan ahead, the outcomes can be less favorable.

For instance, homes in many states usually sell faster and with a little price premium in the spring and summer months as opposed to the winter. If your goal is to get as much as possible for your home, selling during the peak season makes sense.

If you know that your house needs some work and updating in order to sell it for the maximum price, having this planned ahead of time will save you both money and stress. Before you spend any money on your home, call a housing professional and get an expert opinion. By so doing, you will avoid repairing things that do not really need repairing or upgrading a home with the wrong finish for your area.

Having this plan in place ahead of time will save you from pouring your hard-earned money down the drain. On many occasions, our company can buy a senior's home for the price they want and prevent them from having to make any repairs or upgrades. If you know that your house needs a lot of work and you already have an investor set up that you know, like, and trust, the process is much easier when you are ready to move.

Selling Your Home

The decision to sell your home is not necessarily an easy one. Here are a few things to consider:

Finances

Houses cost money, even if they have been paid off. If you have not paid your house off, you have the mortgage payments to deal with, but all homes have maintenance, tax, and insurance costs.

If your house is negatively affecting your finances, this could be a reason to sell it. Property taxes can be a serious problem for seniors who have purchased a home in an area where home prices have greatly increased in value. Many of our customers in such areas are on a fixed budget and cannot manage a large increase in their property tax bills—this is an area where seniors can get into trouble.

Max's grandmother's house was impacted by this. During the last ten years that she lived in the home, the tax value of her property more than doubled. Although she got extra exemptions for being over 65, she still had to pay more in taxes each year. Customers who are unprepared for this—or cannot afford the rising costs—can end up late on their taxes and even risk a tax-related foreclosure if the matter is not addressed.

Mobility

If your mobility is severely restricted, your current home may not be the right fit, which could have a physical, emotional, or mental impact on you. Although she would not come out and say it, Max knew that Grandma was really frustrated by the fact that she could not get around her own house—a house that she loved—the way she wanted to.

Ultimately, she decided not to sell her house, and she lived there until the Lord took her to heaven. However, for some people, a lack of mobility has the greatest impact on their desire or ability to live independently.

Emotional Ties

What is your emotional connection to your home? Whether you have lived in your house for six months or 60 years, your emotional connection to your home impacts on your decision to sell. We often deal with seniors who are living in the house they grew up in.

What memories stand out when you think about the time you have lived in your home? Some customers have a great deal of good memories that keep them from letting go of their homes, whereas some of our seniors have numerous bad memories that they would like to forget.

Is your home a treasure that is hard to part with, or is it something you would like to move on from and forget as quickly as possible?

Spouse

Losing a spouse is a difficult experience. Many of our customers move from their homes because the weight from the memory of losing their spouse in their home is too much to bear.

Are You Really Prepared?

What if your Senior Housing Plan was ready today? Do you know how you will sell your home, who you will sell your home to, and when the plan will start? Are all your family members included in the plan, and is everyone in agreement about what will happen at each point in the journey?

This highlights the benefit of going through these chapters and beginning to start building out your Senior Housing Plan today. We also regularly conduct Senior Planning Workshops for our seniors and their family members.

For more information, reach out to us at www.cabinvestments.com, 708-316-0545, or mikeandmarisa@theseniorhousingbook.com.

One of the greatest gifts you can give to your family is having a plan in place—when (and not if) something changes, your family will be prepared, and they will be so happy that you had the foresight to put things in writing and build out your roadmap.

Remember that you do not have to have everything perfectly planned out; there is no such thing as a perfect plan, but that should never be an excuse to not plan at all.

Creating the Roadmap:
Success Steps

Step 1 – Goals

What are your goals for when you sell your home?

You and your family need to map out what the desired outcome is for the sale of your home. Most goals involve a timeline, the closing or move out process, and the desired price range you will accept for the sale of your home.

Many customers reach out to us and are really not sure about what to expect with regard to areas since it may have been 5, 10, or 20+ years since they have bought or sold a home.

Make sure that you consult with a real estate professional that shares your core values and is someone you know, like, and trust. In addition, make sure that you are working with someone that has real expertise in the area you need help with.

Selling your home and transitioning to a new destination is a major life event. Make sure that you have the right team that can help you with all aspects of this move. To start getting your roadmap planned out today, reach out to us at:

www.cabinvestments.com, 708-316-0545, or mikeandmarisa@theseniorhousingbook.com.

Step 2 – Condition

Another step to successfully selling your home is getting an expert opinion on the condition of your home. Depending on where you live, some homes may sell well in any condition, while others really need to be fixed up to current standards.

When was the last time you remodeled your home? How does the condition of your home compare to the others for sale in your area?

Real estate is very localized, meaning that there can be a big difference in home prices and buyer demand in different states, cities, or neighborhoods. Even in your own neighborhood, it can be very different just one street over. So, when you are working with a real estate professional, make sure that they are an expert in your neighborhood. Choosing the wrong professional or trying to "go it alone" could cost you thousands of dollars, weeks of wasted time, and more stress and heartache.

After getting in touch with us or someone in your local market and having your house evaluated, you should be able to get an idea of its current condition and the implications of this for your plan to sell it.

Remember that when you are trying to sell, it is not about how you evaluate the condition of the home; instead, the sale is based on the perception of buyers in your neighborhood and your local market. It is therefore important to look at the condition of your home through the lens of the buyers and how they will perceive it.

In 2011, when Max's grandmother passed away, the family was in charge of selling her home. In their minds, the condition of her home was great, but local buyers did not feel the same way. They loved Grandma's home and had great memories there. However, the problem was that they were not the people who wanted to buy the house.

After she had bought her home, house values in her neighborhood increased rapidly. In the 1970s, houses in her area would go for upwards of $50,000. However, fast forwarding to the late 2000s, homes before the 2008 crash were going for upwards of $500,000.

Buyers in this area (and at these prices) therefore had very high standards with regard to the finish-out materials and amenities of such a property. Although some updates had been done to the house, most of it was the same as the day it had been bought in 1974.

This can frustrate sellers, who see homes going for high prices in their neighborhood but do not understand why real estate professionals are quoting lower prices. Max's grandmother's house was bought "as-is" for a much lower price than if it had been fully updated. Eventually, the house was torn down and a larger, new home now stands in its place.

Step 3 – The Real Estate Market

As mentioned in the previous section, real estate is very localized, meaning that there are big differences between states, cities, neighborhoods, and even streets.

If you have lived in your house for a long time, you may not be familiar with your local real estate market. We do not have time to teach a whole course on the real estate market, but we are going to cover the most important things you need to know.

For more info, reach out to us at: www.cabinvestments.com, 708-316-0545, or mikeandmarisa@theseniorhousingbook.com.

Market Cycles

We once heard someone say, "The real estate market is like the elevator business—very up and down." Sometimes, it is *easy* to sell your home for a great price, and sometimes it is very *difficult* to sell your home.

We get buyers that are really excited to get a great price for their home, only to find out they really did not gain very much because prices had increased not only for their own homes but also in the places they were moving to.

Partnering with a real estate professional who can help you understand where the market in your local neighborhood is right now will really help to give you an idea of what to do.

In 2011, Max's family was in charge of selling his grandmother's home. It was not a great time to be a seller in their area—foreclosures were very high, and home values were much lower than in the four previous years.

Different strategies work at different points in the real estate cycle. So, knowing these strategies gives you an invaluable advantage when making your plan.

Seller's Market

When you are in a seller's market, homes are in short supply, and there are lots of buyers that want to be in your neighborhood—it is easier to find a buyer. You can get a higher price and usually do not need to do as much updating to the home.

Buyer's Market

When you are in a buyer's market, there are many homes for sale, and buyers are in short supply. That is where we were in 2011—numerous homes were up for sale and no one was buying them.

Homes that are fully fixed-up for a great price normally go first in this type of market. For example, in a seller's market, some buyers will overlook cosmetic updates that are needed since they really want to get into a certain neighborhood and do not have many choices.

In a buyer's market, there are so many houses to choose from, and buyers normally pick the houses that are already updated as opposed to those that need a lot of work. Since there are many housing choices, buyers are not limited to purchasing homes that may need a lot of work.

Max's grandmother's house was not one of those updated homes. After she passed away, it took his family a year to sell her house. They went through multiple real estate agents and different investors. There were a couple of times where they thought they had the house sold, but things kept falling though.

Knowing what your strategy would be if you need to sell during one of these times is important for your outcome.

For more info, reach out to us at: www.cabinvestments.com, 708-316-0545, or mikeandmarisa@theseniorhousingbook.com.

Step 4 – Emotions

To be successful selling your home, you will need to think about your emotions. Emotions are powerful forces subconsciously driving our decisions. The reasons you love your home may not be the same reasons that someone else does. Your emotions, memories, and attachments to the different parts of your home may be the opposite of what the potential buyer is feeling.

If your house needs a lot of updating, you will receive offers that you may interpret as low. You would not know if someone was trying to take advantage of your lack of real estate knowledge or if the "low" offer was really fair.

We try our best to be as sensitive as possible to our customers while also giving them the hard facts about their real estate and its current condition. This is where having an adult child, sibling, or another trusted advisor on your team can really help make these decisions go smoothly. Get someone on your team to lean on instead of doing it all on your own.

Step 5 – Physical Items

If someone needs to move quickly, what is going to happen to all the physical items in the home? If your senior gets sick, who is going to sift through all the items in the home? How long will it take?

Believe it or not, not all senior citizens are minimalistic. Years and decades of memories and special belongings can slowly collect over time, creating an extremely large inventory of physical items to go through, regardless of whether the move is imminent or in the future. Many customers, having spent weeks or even months going through the items in their parents' home, still feel like they are only scratching the surface.

An elderly lady had gone into a nursing home, and her adult son called a real estate agent to take a look at the house. For two months prior to this, her son had been spending nights and weekends cleaning the house.

When the agent walked into the home, he could not see the walls since objects and belongings were stacked all the way to the ceiling, with pathways forged through the items so as to walk to different parts of the house.

He turned to the seller's son and inquired, "Jeff, how are you progressing?"

Jeff replied, "Slowly."

His mom never threw anything away, and now her adult children had to go through it all. This topic could easily have a chapter of its own.

If you have been storing things up, what would happen to all of those items if you were to suddenly pass away or needed to sell your home quickly?

As you create your plan, start thinking about reducing your possessions now. The more streamlined your home becomes, the more you can easily see and enjoy the items you really love (that are currently being hidden by things you just like or tolerate).You will have less to worry about in the future if you have to move quickly or if you move according to your plan.

When our company buys people's homes, we let them leave as many of their physical items as they want. Often, our customers will move with just 10% or 20% of what they had accumulated—or only those things they consider special—to their new house, leaving the rest for us to donate or dispose of. We do not even charge extra for this service—it is an added value that we extend to our customers. A lot of people are not aware that investors tend to do this, so incorporate this into your plan if you are thinking about going down the investor route.

However, if you plan to sell your home to someone who will be moving in, leaving your physical items behind will not be an option. Unless they are buying your furniture, the home will need to be empty.

Ways to Sell Your House

There is no one-size-fits-all approach, so we are going to briefly cover the three main ways you can sell a house later in this chapter and what the benefits and detriments of each one are.

Be cautious of anyone who tells you that their choice is the best in all situations. It depends on many factors that we have already covered in this book and also on what your individual goals are. Our job is not to persuade you to pick one or the other but to give you the information and let you and your team decide what is best for you.

For more information, reach out to us at www.cabinvestments.com, 708-316-0545, or mikeandmarisa@theseniorhousingbook.com.

Mistakes to Avoid

Too many of our potential customers waste time, energy, and money because they do not fully understand how to deal with a home that is no longer serving its purpose. These are the biggest mistakes made by adult family members who are in charge of selling the property.

Mistake #1: Picking the Wrong Person to Take Advice from or Not Taking Advice from Anyone

There are some great real estate professionals in all markets, but finding them requires work. It takes 180 hours of training to pass a real estate license test in our state and to be on the path to becoming a real estate agent.

Compare that to 1,500 hours to get a cosmetology license in the same state. Someone can cut your hair, make a mistake, and your hair will grow back. However, that person has been required to take over eight times as many training hours (800% more!) as someone who could be advising you on one of the largest financial transactions you may ever be involved in (i.e., selling your home).

On the investor side, it can be even worse. There are no licensing requirements for an investor to buy your home from you. You could be working with a very reputable company or be approached by someone who has attended a three-hour weekend class and only knows the basics.

How will you know who to work with? The rest of this chapter and book will provide you with some strategies to help you make the right choices.

Mistake #2: Working Nights and Weekends on Fixing Up a Home with the Goal of Increasing the Purchase Price

This is a default decision for a lot of well-meaning children. People think that if they fix up the house, it will be worth a lot more. Although a fixed-up home can sell for more, the type of repairs and updates you make require a strong knowledge of the local area.

If you update the home with materials that are more expensive than the area requires (over-rehabbing), that extra cost is wasted. If you use materials that are below the neighborhood standard, the buyers will not like it, and you will either not get much for the work or it will have to be redone in order to satisfy potential buyers.

Even if you predict the rehab requirements and repairs 100% correctly, who is going to do the work? If it is you, how long will it take you when compared to a professional, and how much is your time worth? If you are in a full-time job and are trying to help your sick parent, you may not have as much time as you think.

We get customers that find out—after three or more months of work—that their efforts have not yielded the results they had expected. Before starting work on a house, consult a trusted advisor or reach out to your team to help figure out your best strategy.

Option 1 – Sell the House with an Agent

This is how most people sell their fixed-up, fully updated homes. After Max's grandmother passed away, the family sold her house through a real estate agent. It took over a year, a lot of which had to do with the market conditions. In this sense, it was 2011, at the very bottom of the real estate cycle. The home needed a massive amount of work—it had 30 years of deferred maintenance, and not a lot of owner-occupied buyers were buying "as-is" houses.

The family's agent had sold homes in the area before but did not really specialize in selling homes that were in rough shape. Most agents only want to advertise the best-looking houses since their personal brand is affected by the condition and quality of the homes they sell.

The agent did not send out a great deal of marketing materials for the home because an "as-is" older house does not look as good as a fixed-up, gorgeous house. The home was not the kind that fit with her personal brand, and so the family's needs were put onto the back burner.

Below are some sample questions to use when you are interviewing an agent. Each question is accompanied by a short explanation of its importance. We have a preferred, referral list of real estate agents that have agreed to our ethical standards. If you are in need of a real estate agent referral, reach out to us at:

www.cabinvestments.com, 708-316-0545, or mikeandmarisa@theseniorhousingbook.com.

Questions for Real Estate Agents

How Long Have You Been in Business?

This is very important—there is no substitute for experience. Let us emphasize: There is no substitute for experience. There are some "long-time" agents that are not very good at what they do, and there are some unseasoned agents that are very good at what they do.

Experience allows someone to see things differently. However, the kind of experience is just as important. If someone has been in the business for ten years but has only helped a few customers in your situation, that might not be good enough.

In our experience, most motivated, full-time agents have a good amount of knowledge and experience by their second-year anniversary.

Are You Full-Time or Part-Time?

Sometimes, people leave one of the most important financial decisions of their life, i.e., selling a home, to someone who has only sold a couple of homes and only works part time. Would you want a part-time medical doctor who also has a day job in a lumber office until his medical business starts to pick up working on your heart?

Our recommendation is to go with somebody that is full time—they will be more available when you need them and should have more experience. If they are not full time in this business, there is probably a good reason why.

Is the Agent You Are Considering Related to You?

This can be good or bad depending on the situation. Have you ever heard the phrase, "Keep family/friends and business separate?" You need a real estate professional that really knows what they are doing, and you need a real estate professional that knows the local market.

The biggest risk in hiring a family member to represent you is that if things do not go the way you want them to, you would probably not be comfortable firing them, which would be to your own detriment. How would that affect other people in the family?

Some families do not like disclosing or handling money matters with other members of the family.

In some markets, if you sell with an agent, you are going to need to put a lot of work into the house first for it to sell at top dollar. Consider working with the best agent available—not just the best agent you are related to—so that you can recoup what you have invested.

What Neighborhood Do They Specialize in?

Real estate is very localized. What works in one neighborhood may not work in another. Find an agent that really knows your zip code and neighborhood and understands what buyers in that area want.

Have they helped buy or sell a house in your neighborhood in the last 12 months?

If so, what was the outcome?

Can I Contact Your References?

Get some references from people your agent has worked with in the past. How they treated their previous clients is probably how you will be treated.

You do not want to work with an agent that is hard to get hold of when you need them.

Final Thoughts on Using a Real Estate Agent

The decision of whether to use a real estate agent or not can be determined by market conditions, what your needs are, if you have money to put into the house, and how quickly you need to sell your home.

Typical customers that use an agent want to get the absolute most for their home. They are willing to wait a little bit longer if needed for the house to sell, and their homes are either mostly or fully updated. If needed, these customers have the time and money to make repairs or updates as the buyer demands.

If you need a referral, reach out to us at www.cabinvestments.com, 708-316-0545, or mikeandmarisa@theseniorhousingbook.com.

Option 2 – Flip or Update Your Home Before You Sell It

TV shows do a great job of fueling the popularity of this strategy. Beware! Flipping homes like they do on TV is not the same thing as rehabbing your home in real life. If you are going through a situation where your senior has to move quickly, this strategy is no less enticing, but it is much harder to execute.

We rehab many homes each year, and it is a difficult process with many steps. Customers who try to flip their homes on their own are usually not satisfied with the results. What sounds like a good idea at the time rarely leads to the desired outcome.

Sometimes, our customers get halfway through some updates, call us, and sell us the house "as-is." If projects have not been carried out correctly or have only been half done, it can be harder to sell the home than if nothing had been attempted in the first place.

Evelin Needs Good Advice

A customer called and said, "The value of this home is all the money I have for retirement. I am 82 years old, and I have some money to put into the house if it will help sell it for more."

Evelin was told by two real estate agents that she could list the home "as-is" and sell it for $150,000. However, the third agent (full time and on our referral list) listened closely to Evelin's needs.

Evelin was told that she could probably sell the house "as-is" in its current condition for

$150,000. There were some repairs that needed to be done, and it may have taken a little longer to sell because of its condition at the time.

Another option would be investing about $15,000 to update the home, perform some foundation repair, and fix a few cosmetic issues, and she would then be able to sell the house for more. Evelin ended up rehabbing the home with her own money, and she paid our company to do that for her.

After her $15,000 investment, she was able to sell her home for $185,000.

$185,000 - $15,000 = $170,000.

Therefore, Evelin was able to get about $20,000 more for her home with this strategy. She was no longer living in the house, and she had $15,000 to pay for repairs. The closing process did take about two months longer, and she did have to deal with some stress.

You are not going to get something for nothing, but it was worth it to the customer in this case. It was possible that the housing market could have started to slow down or prices could have dropped quickly while she was still fixing it up, thereby impacting on her profitability. However, these were risks that Evelin was willing to take.

When It Does Not Go as Planned

Sally was 78 years old and lived by herself. She had experienced a fall and no longer felt safe living alone. Beth, Sally's oldest daughter, called one of our real estate offices. Her mom had fallen down again and was now in a physical therapy facility. Beth did not expect her mom to be able to move back into her house.

The plan was to move her into an assisted care facility. Beth was asking about what they should do with Sally's home. She told us that they had thought about updating the house and then flipping it. Beth and her husband both had full-time jobs and lived about 20 miles from the home.

They were thinking about putting in some floors, replacing the windows, and painting the inside and outside of the house so that they could sell it for more money. If you are a contractor with lots of extra time and money for materials, this may be a great option.

The real estate agent asked Beth how much time she needed each week to take care of her family (she still had teenage kids at home) and check on her mom. Beth had a limited capacity for handling all these demands. We do not recommend people to rehab their homes when they are in the middle of a medical crisis with a family member.

For more info, reach out to us at: www.cabinvestments.com, 708-316-0545, or mikeandmarisa@theseniorhousingbook.com.

Value Is Not the Same

Remember that every neighborhood is unique. The right flooring or finishes in your neighborhood may be a waste of time and money in a different neighborhood.

Certain repairs increase the value of your home much more than others. For example, if you replace the air conditioning unit, you will normally get a small premium above what you paid. People like to have a new air conditioning unit, but it is not going to yield a lot when compared to the cost.

Putting in a $5,000 air conditioner will not increase the value of a home by $15,000. The math is more like a $5,000 air conditioner increasing the value by $5,000 or $6,000 and usually helping the home to sell faster. In this sense, you will typically have to invest $5,000 to make $0–$1000 on the purchase price after factoring in the cost.

The Speed of the Repair Work

If you are doing updates to the home, you probably do not have as much time to devote to it as a full-time contractor would, or you would work a whole lot slower than a contractor (or perhaps both). While it might take a three-man crew (charging $400) one day to put the flooring in, it may take you three days, seven days, or even a whole month.

Do you want to invest your time and energy in fixing up a home or spending it with your loved ones? Your loved one may have just gone into an assisted living facility or some type of senior facility. No one lives forever—the average stay in an assisted living center in the United States is around 28 months.[2]

Our recommendation is that you do not work on the floor and you do not paint the house—spend time with your aging relative instead. If you rehab your own home, just remember that your return on time invested is not going to be very high, unless you are an expert.

Leave rehabbing homes to the professionals.

For more info, reach out to us at: www.cabinvestments.com, 708-316-0545, or mikeandmarisa@theseniorhousingbook.com.

---

[2] Source: "So I'll Probably Need Long-Term Care, But for How Long? *MyLifeSite*, 28 June 2018. Retrieved from www.mylifesite.net/blog/post/so-ill-probably-need-long-term-care-but-for-how-long/

Option 3 – Sell to an Investor

A good real estate investment company will share your core values and provide you with a real service. Make sure to find companies that have high standards. Remember that just like real estate agents and contractors, real estate investors seek to make a profit from their work. Real estate investors take the most risk in regard to all the aforementioned categories.

A real estate agent can tell you that your house will sell for any amount you want to hear. When the house does not sell for a certain amount, they can drop the price. A contractor is working on your house but is not taking the risk of selling it. A real estate investor is going to buy your house and take all the rehab and selling risks.

Normally, you get the least amount for your home when you sell to an investor. The investor is not going to live in the home, so the home is not worth as much to them as to someone who will. Also, the investor is going to spend months and tens or hundreds of thousands of dollars improving the home.

One of our real estate partners recently bought a fixed-up home from a customer. Since the house was fixed up and in wonderful shape, they told the customer that they would net out more money if they sold their home with a real estate agent or to someone who was going to live in it. However, the downside would be that it would take longer, and they would have to open their home to showings and possibly deal with any repairs that may be needed after the inspection process.

Although their all-cash offer was $11,000 less than the best estimate of selling through an agent, the customer chose the offer instead. She and her husband were moving to a 55+ independent living community and did not want the hassle of selling her home as the slower winter season approached. She said, "I can get more money; I cannot get any more time."

Selling to an investor does have benefits. Customers who are a good fit for this generally want or need to sell their homes quickly. Typically, this involves a completed closing in less than 30 days from going under contract.

Ideal customers for this option are those who do not have a lot of money to put into the house for repairs or updates. Other instances are where the house is in rough shape or has a fair amount of deferred maintenance.

Our ideal customers are seniors in this situation. We do work with other age groups, but our focus and specialty is helping seniors get the best advice for their unique situation.

For more info, reach out to us at: www.cabinvestments.com, 708-316-0545, or mikeandmarisa@theseniorhousingbook.com.

Questions for Real Estate Investors

Here are some questions you can ask a potential real estate investor.

How Do You Come Up with a Fair Price for the Home?

This does not have to be your first question, but it is obviously something that is on everybody's mind. The biggest problem with the term "fair price" is a fair price for whom? In this regard, a "fair price" normally represents a range. A customer wants to get as much as they can for their house, and a business wants to make as much as it can for its bottom line.

It seems like the customer and investor are on opposing sides, like soldiers in battle using any advantage to gain a better position. There is a way to engage in this price topic so that the customer and company are on the same side.

Max worked as a math teacher for seven years, so whenever he discusses price with customers, his thought process encompasses the following criteria:

1. The price has to be a win-win for both parties.

2. There are other things to consider besides just price.

3. An educated customer is a more comfortable, happier customer.

The Price Has to Be a Win-Win for Both Parties

The homeowner needs to get a fair price they are happy with. The price should reflect the current condition of the home and what is involved (time, energy, and money) to get the home to market standards. The person who does that work (the investor) needs to make a fair profit for that type of risk.

The fastest way to get the price you want for your home is to tell the person who is interested either what you want for the home or what you think is a fair price. The second step is being open to information about the true fair market value of your home.

Sometimes, customers are afraid to say what they really want for their house, thinking that it will be lower than what an investor is thinking about offering. Nine times out of ten, however, the number the customer wants is higher than the true value. Communicating this to your investor is a great way not to waste time and move on to finding the right solution for you.

Things to Consider Other Than Price

Price is important, but what about time and energy? How much is your time worth? The most important thing to consider (other than price) is who you are working with. If someone says they are going to buy your house for a great-sounding number but they never show up at the closing, what was that great number really worth? Nothing!

Educated Customers

If you do not know anything about home values and repair costs, it will be difficult to know what a fair offer is. Since our company was founded by teachers, we teach our customers what is going on in their areas and let them figure out what is fair to them.

We have all heard investor horror stories. We have personally seen investors walk into a house, give a customer an offer, and then ask them to accept it. How can you accept an offer if you do not know what it is based on?

Our Process

When it comes to price, our team educates our customers on what their house would sell for in an "as-is" state when compared to other houses sold in similar conditions.

We do not base our values on what the neighbor thinks their house is worth, what a friend at church who almost has a real estate license imagines it is worth, or what houses sold for at some point in the area. We look at homes that have sold recently in your area.

For more info, reach out to us at: www.cabinvestments.com, 708-316-0545, or mikeandmarisa@theseniorhousingbook.com.

Example

Based on homes that were sold in your area, let us conservatively estimate that your home would sell for $150,000, fully fixed-up and updated.

Conservatively, with overages accounted for, let us say that it would take a professional $50,000 to get the home to this type of condition.

$150,000 - $50,000 = $100,000.

This is not the price an investor can pay for your home because there are other costs involved, and the investor needs to make a profit for their work (just like you get paid when you go to work).

Why the Investor Needs to Make a Profit

- Working on a house and doing investment work carries a great deal of risk. For example, house prices could go down by the time the investor sells the home.

- The cost of the rehab could go a lot higher, so all that has to be built into the margin. When you see an investor making a $20,000 or $30,000 profit on a flipped home, some people think that is not fair and that they have also been ripping others off. Max used to think that way when he was a math teacher helping to sell his grandmother's house. Investing has the potential for gains and losses.

- An investor can make money, but they can also lose money. In 2008, many local investors could not sell their properties. As a result, many lost them and went out of business. In this regard, a lot of the foreclosures in the last recession did not only happen to homeowners but also to investors.

- There are factors you cannot see that affect the value of your home. Are there termites in the walls or under the pier and beam foundations? Is there an undiscovered plumbing issue that could cost an additional $10,000 to fix? Is there mold in the bathroom that needs special services to treat? If an old home is being sold, there are things no one knows about until repairs start. Do you want to take that risk on or do you want to transfer that risk to an investor?

Questions for Potential Investor Buyers

How Are You Going to Pay for the House?

Not everyone who says, "I pay cash for houses" is actually going to buy your home. There is a business out there right now called wholesaling.

Wholesaling

A wholesaler is an investor that gets your home under contract for an agreed-upon price and then sells the contract to a cash buyer for more money.

Example

You call the number on a sign that says, "Jesse buys houses," and Jesse comes over and agrees to buy your home for $100,000. He may or may not tell you that he has no plans to buy your home with cash and actually does not have the ability to do so.

Jesse tells you that he needs to have some of his "partners" or "contractors" come over to the house to look at it before the closing. He may even ask to have an open house to show the property to them. What Jesse is really doing is having real cash buyers come over to buy the house from him for $110,000.

A cash buyer who likes the home will agree to buy the property from Jesse for $110,000, and Jesse "assigns" the contract to the cash buyer. At the closing, if all goes according to plan, the cash buyer will pay $110,000 for the house, the customer will receive $100,000, and the wholesaler—Jesse—will receive $10,000.

What would have happened if you worked with the cash buyer directly? Would you have received $10,000 more?

Wholesaling has come under fire from some states because people who do it the wrong way can end up misleading customers.

If Jesse came to your home and told you, "I am not going to buy the house, but I am going to introduce this home to my large list of cash buyers. One of them is going to buy your house, and I am going to make a profit off of that," then that is fine as long as you get the price you want for your home and you know what is going on. If Jesse is adding value for you, there is nothing wrong with him getting paid.

For more info, reach out to us at: www.cabinvestments.com, 708-316-0545, or mikeandmarisa@theseniorhousingbook.com.

Beware of the Inexperienced Wholesaler

The problem is when an inexperienced wholesaler gets your home under contract (control) and is not able to sell it because of a lack of experience. Some new investors start out wholesaling.

Some companies buy and later sell properties without working on them. The difference is that they always purchase the home with their cash and then sell them after the homeowner has been paid. New wholesalers may never buy your home even though some seem like they are going to

One of our partner real estate offices offered to buy a home for $75,000, and the customer told them that another investor had offered $85,000. However, that investor was a new wholesaler who did not really know what he was doing. The wholesaler filled out a contract to purchase it but was not really going to. Three days later, this wholesaler called the office asking if they wanted to buy the home.

After three weeks, the wholesaler canceled the contract because he was unable to sell the home to anyone else. There were a couple of clauses in the contract that allowed him to cancel with no penalty.

The homeowner thought that their house had been sold and had already started to move out. They were counting on the money from the closing to put down on another place to live. They ended up calling the real estate office, and the home was sold in less than seven days.

Proof of Funds

Do not be afraid to request a proof of funds letter, even if it is from investors. A proof of funds letter is issued by a bank or financial institution and shows how a person can actually pay for the house. The investor can also show you a bank statement as financial proof.

If I Do Repairs to the House, Can That Increase the Value and by How Much?

Most investors can get the work done on houses much cheaper than a homeowner can.

When a customer does the work on a house that they are going to sell to an investor, it is usually not worth the time, energy, or money.

For more info, reach out to us at: www.cabinvestments.com, 708-316-0545, or mikeandmarisa@theseniorhousingbook.com.

In What Condition Can We Leave the House if We Sell It to You?

A lot of customers do not know that most investors will not charge them any extra for leaving items in their home. If there is furniture left behind, extra clothes in the closet, or some junk in the shed, ask the investor if their price includes leaving all of these things behind?

Usable items that have been left behind can be donated to local charities like Habitat for Humanity or women's shelters. We do not charge our customers any extra to do this. Instead of spending days, nights, and weekends cleaning out each square foot of the house, they can just leave those items behind.

If you are selling a house to an investor and there are other important events going on, you want to be present and focused on them—do not clean out the whole house if you do not have to.

When Can We Close?

This is obviously important if you are selling the home to pay for another home or medical bills. Most investors can close on a home within 30 days or sooner depending on the condition of the title.

We pay all the closing costs for our customers. The only things our customers are responsible for are the taxes they owe on the property and any liens or mortgages.

Do You Have Any References?

You can read their reviews online (e.g., Home Advisor, Angie's List, and The Good Contractor's List), look them up on social media (e.g., Facebook and LinkedIn), or check them out with the Better Business Bureau. These are good starting points, but they rarely tell the whole story.

A dentist recently extracted six teeth from a patient's mouth. She needed his help but did not have a lot of money, so he worked on her at a discount. The following day, after the procedure, she wrote a mediocre review of his practice because her mouth still hurt.

As long as a business owner pays monthly fees to be in the Better Business Bureau and responds to any complaints, the owner will keep an "A" rating. Talking over the phone to actual customers is a better strategy to gauge if this is the right company for you.

Will You Need Access to the Property?

Investors may want to have their contractors come over and take a look at the house in order to start ordering materials. Sometimes, we restrict access to the vacant property with a lockbox that has a code only known to us and the customer.

When Will the Utilities and Insurance Be Cut Off?

Utilities and insurance for the house should be terminated on the closing date. After the closing is complete and the purchase has been funded, it is safe to turn off the utilities and cancel the insurance.

What Does the Closing Process Look Like?

Closing processes vary from one state to the next. Use a firm that is reputable, and never perform a closing anywhere except from an attorney's office or a title company. If somebody wants to do a closing at the kitchen table, get some legal advice and double-check it first.

Make sure that you understand what costs you are responsible for. When we buy a customer's home, we pay all the closing costs.

Read the fine print so that you know exactly what you are going to be paying for. Sometimes, an investor may be paying for half of the closing costs instead of 100%.

Who Pays Additional Lawyer's or Closing Costs?

If there are additional closing costs because of a probate or other legal issue, know who is going to be responsible for paying these costs.

For more info, reach out to us at: www.cabinvestments.com, 708-316-0545, or mikeandmarisa@theseniorhousingbook.com.

Power of Attorney

If someone with a power of attorney is involved, make sure that all relevant documents are presented to the title company or attorney.

The title company will review the documents, sign off that the documents are valid, and verify that the person has the power to sell the home. A lawyer can also tell you if the documents are too old or have not been prepared well.

If the documents are not valid, you need to find that out as soon as possible so that the closing will not be delayed.

Things to Watch Out for

An Agent that Prices the House Too High

This can happen for a number of reasons. It is difficult to know exactly what the perfect price for a house will be.

Sometimes, a seller wants a certain price and the real estate agent does not challenge them; another reason could be a change in the market; finally, everyone could have just been overly optimistic.

Once you list your home on the multiple listing service (MLS), that price is on record. If you have to lower the price, it can make your listing look weak and cause offers to come in lower than expected.

Selling a House with an Agent – Picky Buyers

When you accept a buyer's purchase contract, the buyer has a certain number of days to get an inspection report completed (normally three to seven days). The buyer then has the option to cancel the contract or keep everything in place.

After looking at the inspection report, the buyer could ask you to carry out a lot of repairs or substantially lower the price.

Selling a House with an Agent –The House Does Not Appraise

In a seller's market, the prices of homes can be higher than they have ever been. Before a loan is approved, the bank or financial institution orders an independent appraisal of the property.

Sometimes, the appraiser who places the value on the home will not value it as highly as the purchase price amount. The buyer can still buy your home, but they are going to have to make up the difference with their own money.

House Did Not Appraise

One of our partner companies was selling a home that they had under contract to sell for $210,000. The appraiser came through seven days before they were scheduled to close and said that the home was only worth $200,000.

The company was in a quandary—they could not close unless the buyer came up with $10,000 in cash. In some markets, the buyers have the cash, but they sometimes do not want to use it. In the end, they had to lower the price, and the buyer put in some cash to make it happen. The closing stayed on schedule, but there were some bumps along the way.

Selling to an Investor – Foreclosure Deadline

We help customers in different stages of the foreclosure process. A foreclosure can be from a mortgage company that is yet to receive a past due amount, from outstanding taxes owed, and in some states from defaulting on a reverse mortgage loan.

When you do not pay a loan back on time, the mortgagee has the right to force the sale of your home. Unfortunately, when seniors sometimes get into this situation, they get nervous, freeze up, and do nothing.

They are afraid to tell their family members what is going on financially, and the situation just gets worse. Customers often reach out to us and our partner companies to sell their homes two or three days before the foreclosure auction. Sometimes, they can be helped, but this is sometimes not possible because they are out of time.

We recommend that you talk to your team of advisors (accountant and attorney) and call your lender to try to work something out. Do this as soon as you think you may miss a payment. If you are in a tough situation, most companies will work with you. If too much time has passed before you pay, or if you do not contact them, the creditor will not be as flexible.

Decision Time

So, how will you know if it is time to make a decision? Go through the steps in this guide and consult your team.

It might be time to wait.

It might be the time to sell now.

Contact Us

Whether you need or want to sell your home (or are thinking about it), reach out to us at:

www.cabinvestments.com, 708-316-0545, or mikeandmarisa@theseniorhousingbook.com.

We would love to talk to you and help you understand all your options. We are in business to help seniors—this is why our business exists. We also have Senior Planning Workshops for seniors and their family members. reach out to us today to register for one of these workshops.

There is never any cost to attend. This workshop is about education and helping your family prepare for tomorrow. You will receive a

Senior Planning Workbook for free. All of our attendees will also receive a copy of this book.

Chapter Goal

Our goal for this chapter has been to help you better understand all the factors that go into deciding whether or not you even want to sell your home and some of the ways by which to sell your home.

Planning ahead is the key. Feel free to reach out to us to start the planning process today.

Home To Home

Chapter 4: Keeping Your Home and Staying in It

Recently, a customer (Mark) called one of our partner offices and told them that his mom, Betty, was probably better off selling her home, and he wanted some advice on their options.

The real estate agent they talked to decided to have all the stakeholders (mom, the three adult children, and the agents) meet at the house so that they could go over all the options. When the agents got to the house, Betty met them at the door and told them that they might as well go home.

Looking confused, one of the agents asked Mark what he wanted them to do. "Let us all go in and talk," Mark replied.

They all went in and gathered around the kitchen table. Betty lived alone, and she needed some extra help with the house. It was literally falling apart. Mark had a pretty demanding job, and he lived about 30 miles away.

When Mark talked to Betty about how he was concerned for her safety, Betty retorted: "Well, there is no way I am ever leaving this house!"

This story plays out every day in our market and all over the United States. Betty wanted to keep her home, so the agent's job was to help them come up with ideas and solutions that could help her do just that. In this sense, their goal was to help her stay in her home and not only make sure she was safe and happy but that her son was also reassured.

It is hard to make everyone happy.

Betty was still of sound mind, so even if the choice was unpopular with her family, it was hers to make. Interestingly enough, within three months of helping her family build out a plan to help Betty stay in the home, her health declined, and she moved into an assisted living facility.

Throughout this chapter, we discuss how to build out a roadmap for staying in your home as long as you want.

The Main Issue

Customers who want to keep their home either want to:

1. Stay in the home, even if their health is failing; or

2. Keep the home in the family, allow another relative to live in it, or pass it down to a son or daughter.

These are separate (sometimes closely connected) issues, so we will spend time discussing each one. If you want to learn how these issues weave into your Senior Housing Plan, reach out to us at:

www.cabinvestments.com, 708-316-0545, or mikeandmarisa@theseniorhousingbook.com.

Staying in your home—even when your health is failing—and passing your home down to your family members are both possible outcomes. The sooner you plan for these events, the better the outcome will be.

The Two Non-Negotiables

Staying in your home has two major components. There are needs emanating from the person that lives in the home, such as safety and security, and the responsibilities of homeownership, such as maintenance and financial obligations.

If you can meet both of these needs, staying in the home can be a great option. If one of these needs cannot be met, staying in your home may not be the best option.

Keeping your home in the family is very possible, but different challenges exist. Whether someone is living in the home or it is vacant, the taxes, mortgage, and insurance need to be paid and kept current. To stay out of trouble with code enforcement and keep the value of the property up, maintenance schedules will also need to stay current.

Leaving a house vacant for a long period of time is not a good idea; a vacant house can become a target for break-ins or other crimes (e.g., vandalism). In addition, maintenance schedules can fall off, leading to major problems with systems in the home.

Lastly, a home that is vacant seems to age faster than a home that is lived in. We do not have any research studies to cite, but when we go into a home that has not been lived in for months or even years, its condition seems to have gone downhill rapidly.

Keeping your home is a lot more complicated than selling it. When you sell your home, you do not have to worry about it anymore after the closing— the pros and cons of owning that home are now someone else's concern.

The path you go down will be up to your individual goals. The goal of this chapter is to give you some things to think about as you craft your plan.

Questions to Think About

1. What recent event has you thinking about staying in your home?

2. What recent event makes keeping your home a concern or a challenge?

3. If your health condition changes, how will you be able to stay in your home? What changes would you need to make to your home?

Max's grandmother was one of those seniors who would not leave her home. She often said to her family, "Under no circumstances would I ever go into a nursing home."

Fortunately, rather than having bossy family members, she had supportive ones. Max's parents felt the same way that she did. When the day came that she needed some extra help, one of her family members moved in with her until her passing. Sometimes, it does not take a health change for there to be a concern about keeping your home.

Home Maintenance

If the homeowner traditionally took care of the home but now has a loss in mobility, maintenance can be quite a big issue

When a homeowner starts experiencing limited mobility, maintenance on the home will be impacted; when maintenance starts to become neglected, conditions in the home can quickly spiral out of control.

Hopefully, you are getting this book early in your senior housing journey, you live in a beautiful, well-maintained house, and you are ready to map out your plans to stay in it.

Who Wants to Buy the Home

If you are in the early stage of planning, ask your family members if anybody wants to buy the house or live in the house when it is time for the senior to leave. If you do not ask, you will not know—never assume anything, and involve all the stakeholders when you start your plan.

There are two components to buying a house: if the buyer is a family member, they need to have the desire and capacity to buy the home.

If a family member is really excited about buying the home but has neither the money nor sufficient credit, that is a capacity issue. If your family member does not have the capacity to buy a stranger's house on your street, you should probably not sell them your house.

For more info, reach out to us at: www.cabinvestments.com, 708-316-0545, or mikeandmarisa@theseniorhousingbook.com.

Sudden Illness

A certain senior fell down while she was at home and needed to be hospitalized. Her son held on to the hope that his mom would make a full recovery and then return home.

After about six months, the family realized that their mom would not be fully independent again or able to return home. During this six-month period, her son worked during the day, attended to his home and family, and visited his mom in the physical therapy rehab center in the evenings; at the weekend, he would take care of his mom's house.

That schedule was exhausting. It was really hard for him to accept that things were no longer going to be the way they were before. He had grown up in the home, and he loved it. His mom told him that she wanted to go back to her home when she got better.

Many questions still needed to be answered.

When will mom get well enough to leave the current facility?

If mom gets healthy again, who will help her at home?

What things need to be done to the house now and in the future in order to keep it up?

Timeline

If you are a senior that currently needs help with mobility and your current home is not meeting your needs, you need to figure out a plan right now.

If your home is vacant and your goal is to pass it on to someone in your family, you do not have to solve the problem with as much urgency; however, as mentioned earlier, you do not want to leave the home vacant for too long.

Build a Roadmap for Keeping Your Home

❑ Do not wait until it is too late.

❑ Who Do not wait until somebody gets sick.

❑ Do not wait until somebody has to move in to a nursing home to figure out what the plan is.

❑ Do it now.

❑ Use the checklists and questions in this chapter to start a discussion and put your plan in place.

For more information, reach out to us at: www.cabinvestments.com, 708-316-0545, or mikeandmarisa@theseniorhousingbook.com.

Benefits of Solving Early

There are three major benefits from having a well-thought-out plan to keep your home:

1. Maintaining the value of your home.

2. Getting the right help you need.

3. Creating a smooth transition.

Maintaining the Value of Your Home

If the plan is to keep your home, you will want to preserve as much of the house's market value as possible. Why would you care about the market value of the home if you are not going to sell it?

Your plan right now may be to keep your house forever, but plans sometimes change. If you need to get a different level of care, that could be expensive. You might need to sell your home in order to pay for your care.

Keeping your home in a condition that will attract the highest market value will be very beneficial.

Access to Future Capital

Suppose you needed to borrow money in the future. There are ways to do that against the appraised value of your house, some of which we will discuss in later chapters. However, the higher the value of your house, the more available funds you will have access to.

Homeownership is one of the biggest net worth components for many Americans, especially when the homeowner has paid off the home. The next section will help shed some light on how to keep both the condition and value of your property up.

The Property Condition

A lot of our seniors let maintenance slide as their expenses increase and their income stays fixed.

For example, suppose a bathroom stops working and there is one senior living in the home. If they are on a fixed budget, and it is going to cost $1,500 to get the bathroom fixed, our senior has two choices: fix it and keep the value up on the house or just leave it alone and not mess with it.

If there is another bathroom in the house, they may start using that one instead of spending money on fixing their other bathroom. Similar isolated events can build up slowly over a 10- or 15-year period, and when the senior goes to sell their home or start getting work done to it, those little projects have turned into seven or eight big projects.

We call this deferred maintenance. So, if your plan is to keep your home, make sure that you set a realistic budget for the monthly and yearly maintenance in order to make sure that you can afford it.

How much should you budget each year for maintenance? Set aside 1 to 3% of the total value of the home for maintenance every year. If you have a $200,000 house, you can expect to spend about $2,000 to $6,000 a year in annual maintenance for the home.

Say your home is a little bit older, and you think you will be closer to the 3% number. If your yearly maintenance bill was estimated at $4,800 a year, that would break down to $400 a month.

You can create a savings account and set up an automatic transfer each month that transfers $400 from your checking account to your home maintenance savings account.

Therefore, say you have a $4,000 plumbing emergency ten months into the year, you will have an emergency fund set up and—instead of using credit cards to maintain your home—you will have the cash available to pay for the repair.

Major System Costs

Every major component of the home has a certain lifespan. Have you ever said to someone, "They do not make them like they used to."

That is a true statement today.

Below are some rough estimates of how long the major systems of your home can last and what they typically cost to replace. There are many factors that affect lifespan and cost—use these as the starting point for your budget.

Roof Replacement

This depends on where you live; however, a new roof should last anywhere from 10 to 20+ years. In southern states, a 30-year roof rarely makes it that long since hailstorms and the intense summer heat chew roofs up quickly. Northern states get tons of snow every year, and while we have no idea what that does to a roof, all that snow is scary.

A typical new roof on a 1,800 square foot home will cost anywhere from $6,000 to $12,000.

For more info, reach out to us at: www.cabinvestments.com, 708-316-0545, or mikeandmarisa@theseniorhousingbook.com.

Foundation Repair

Homeowners can encounter a lot of problems from damaged foundations. Not only is foundation work expensive, but a poor foundation also affects other areas of the home. Many of our customers' homes have visible cracks on the drywall inside the house.

A poor performing foundation can cause plumbing problems; in turn, plumbing problems can cause foundation problems.

If you start seeing cracks on the outside of your house or large cracks on your interior walls, you may have a foundation issue.

We recommend you get an inspection from a licensed structural engineer who is familiar with your area. A structural engineer is not selling you foundation work; their job is to see if there is active movement in your home and then to come up with a plan to fix it.

Foundation repair can range anywhere from $4,000 to over $10,000.

HVAC

Your modern HVAC (heating, ventilation, and air conditioning) system normally lasts between 8 to 12 years. Older units seem to last longer, but every machine has an expiration date. Most of the time, these systems tend to break down in the middle of the summer, when it is 104° outside.

Budget accordingly. Customers who regularly change their air filters (monthly) and get their units serviced each year have reported a much longer lifespan for their equipment.

The cost to replace HVAC equipment (inside and outside) ranges from $6,000 to $10,000.

Plumbing

When it comes to plumbing, there is a wide range with regard to what can go wrong and what the costs can be. If your whole house has ever flooded due to a sewer backup or a busted hot water heater, you will know what we mean. Repairs can range from a leaky faucet to sewer pipe replacement.

Max's grandmother received an unusually large water bill one month. As a result, she got suspicious and had a plumber test the water and sewer system—there was a slab leak at her home.

The pipes under the house had a crack and were leaking water, which caused the soil to swell up and buckle the foundations. When the foundations buckled, it damaged the walls. As a result, some doors could not be opened while others could not be shut. Yikes!

The plumbers carried out a leak isolation test and located the issue. The homeowners insurance did not cover all of the costs, and she was a few thousand dollars out of pocket after it was all done. Plumbing repair can range anywhere from $200 (for someone to come out and fix something basic) to over $10,000 (if you need a new sewer pipe).

Electrical

If you do not add any new outlets or lights, your electrical system should be pretty low maintenance. If you have an original electrical panel that is out of code or has aluminum wiring, look into getting those items replaced and up to the current standards.

At the very least, have your system inspected by a licensed electrician to make sure that you and your home are safe.

Minor things that will require repairs can happen to any system. If you want to add extra lights or outlets to your existing system, make sure that your electrical box can handle the increased load.

The normal cost for electrical repairs ranges from $150 (to get someone out for a small repair) to around $2,000 (to replace an electrical panel) and can exceed $7,000 (if you need to rewire the house with copper to replace old aluminum wiring).

Max and his siblings loved going to Grandma's house, but it required a lot of maintenance to keep it going. Make sure that you have the right amount set aside in your budget to keep both your maintenance and property value up.

For more info, reach out to us at: www.cabinvestments.com, 708-316-0545, or mikeandmarisa@theseniorhousingbook.com.

Getting the Right Help You Need

If you are in the fast-track planning mode, what are your next steps?

Suppose there is a sickness or sudden health crisis and you cannot function in your home as well as you used to. Addressing this situation right away is more important than the value of your house. You want to be able to live as comfortably and safely in your home as possible.

If you plan early, you can start thinking about who in the family might be able to help in the short term. Also, think about what local resources and agencies are available to provide you with help in your home if needed.

Max's grandmother's sickness began suddenly, and he had not started his senior planning pilgrimage yet. In fact, the family in general had not started planning—they probably did not even want to think about it. However, it was something that had a high probability of happening.

In retrospect, he would have planned more. This is one of the main reasons why he got involved in writing this book—to help others put a great plan in place in order to create smooth transitions and favorable outcomes. Fortunately, they had a great family member who stopped what she was doing in order to live with Grandma for a couple of months.

A few months later, Max's grandmother passed away in her home. The family member who was taking care of her admitted that her back was starting to give out. If she had needed care for many more months or years, the family would have had to come up with a different plan. They may have had to sell the house to pay for an outside care facility.

However, at that point, they could have run into a few hurdles:

1. There were no documents created ahead of time to give any family member the power to sell the house while she was still alive.

2. There was a lot of deferred maintenance on the home.

3. At the time, they were in a really bad market to sell her home.

Extra Help

Extra help can range from mobility aids like ramps instead of stairs, help with meal preparation, and transportation to doctor appointments. If you plan to stay in your home and need this type of extra help, who is going to assist you with these needs?

Max's mother was amazing at taking his grandmother to all of her doctor's appointments and running all her errands. They also had a great local grocery store that would deliver groceries to their senior customers. Nowadays, food delivery is very popular, but it was almost non-existent back then.

For more info, reach out to us at: www.cabinvestments.com, 708-316-0545, or mikeandmarisa@theseniorhousingbook.com.

Creating A Smooth Transition

Creating a smooth transition refers to addressing immediate concerns and then setting up the plan for the future. Here are a few questions to help with this:

Immediate Concerns

- If there is a health or mobility issue, who is the caretaker or assistant going to be?

- What steps will you follow to find the right caretaker to help you in your home?

- Who is going to help with the home maintenance?

Planning for the Future

- How is this home going to be passed on?

- Who will take future ownership of your home, and when will it happen?

- Who will be in charge of this process?

- Has this process been documented in collaboration with an attorney?

Legal Matters

You have probably read about this in the news—a celebrity, with access to finances and attorneys, passes away without putting a simple will together. Consult an attorney and get these documents together today. Some of our customers do not create a will, trust, or other planning documents because they think they are too expensive.

How much is it worth to have your plans laid out and followed during difficult times? These documents are not an expense but an investment. There are professionals that work with people on a budget; however, do not make your decision purely on price.

Max's grandmother used an attorney who was affordable, but he did not have the best reputation. She created a trust so that her assets would not have to go through the probate process but would pass smoothly to her heirs.

A will goes through the county probate process and is contestable (challengeable) in court. A will and all the assets in it also become public record. The problem was that the attorney who created the trust did not do a good job, and the trust was not valid. His family did not know that the trust was poorly constructed until after she had passed away.

Fortunately, she had an old will that the family got probated. Her estate was settled, but it took a lot more time and effort than if the plan had been set up correctly from the beginning.

For more info, reach out to us at: www.cabinvestments.com, 708-316-0545, or mikeandmarisa@theseniorhousingbook.com.

What Is the Problem Costing You?

Keeping a home or not keeping a home is a very personal choice that depends on a lot of factors. Paying someone to maintain an older home can get pretty expensive, especially if you are on a fixed budget.

Some make their decision based upon their emotions and feelings about their home, whereas others choose to keep their homes because they cannot afford a senior living facility.

Time is another factor to take into consideration with regard to keeping your home. No matter how much money you have, you cannot get any more time. How much time are you going to be spending at your home? Is it a comfortable and safe place to live? The golden years are supposed to be fun, and your residence is supposed to be an exciting part of your adventure, where you can feel safe and enjoy your life.

Relationships will be impacted upon by your housing decision. When you are thinking about selling or keeping your home, you may notice relatives you have not seen in years showing up to give you advice. Figure out who is really looking out for your best interests and only have those people on your team.

About three years before Max's grandmother passed away, some of her adult children showed up unannounced at her house. However, they were not there to wish her happy birthday or to spend time with her. Instead, they tried to convince her to sell her house and move into a senior housing facility. They told her that the house was too much for her to keep up with and that her family around her was up to some kind of funny business.

She stayed in her home. The craziest part is that the family around her never told her what to do but that she should do whatever she needed. Those adult children that showed up lived far away and never did anything to help her; they only tried to boss her around.

This story is tame compared to others that have been shared by countless seniors. Expect the unexpected! Be careful who you share your plans with. Keep them on a need to know basis. Communicate them to your inner circle, and leave it at that.

The Perfect World

You have your plan in place.

You have made the necessary modifications to your home, or you know who is going to make them. You have set up your maintenance team, yard crew, handyman, and tree-trimming person, and you have completed all your legal documents. You have attended our Senior Planning Workshop. You are in a great position. You can worry less and enjoy more.

Step 1 – Keeping Up the Home

At this point, you have a budget for your yearly maintenance and have set up a separate savings account for it. You have a team of professionals ready to call if something comes up while you are living there.

If your home is vacant and the goal is to pass the home on to the next generation, the challenges are different. If you are taking care of a vacant house, perform regular maintenance as if someone were living there.

If you have a family member that you know, like, and trust, have them live there so that they can keep an eye on the home and help maintain it, even if they only live there part of the week.

Step 2 – Retrofitting the Home

You can modify your existing home to make it more functional for yourself. Max's grandmother added some things to her house to make it easier for her to move around: she used an electric scooter in the house to get around on her own, in addition to adding handrails, ramps, and other mobility aids.

Modifying a home can be expensive up front, but it can be a lot cheaper than moving into an assisted living center. Moreover, staying in your home can be less burdensome than moving in with a family member.

Consult a specialist in senior home modifications. The National Association of Home

Builders has a certification: *Certified Aging-In-Place Specialist*. For more info, visit *www.nahb.org*.

These specialists understand the unique needs of seniors and can make the home modifications you need. When you are getting quotes and bids to make changes to your home—whether it is creating a walk-in shower, adding handrails, or whatever you need to make life a little easier—here are some tips on how to tackle these projects.

Contractor Tips

Make sure you are interviewing contractors that are insured and bonded. This helps protect you in case the contractor makes a mistake on the home or breaks something.

The best contractors are those that are referred by friends and family. It helps your odds if someone you know had a great experience with them.

Make sure that you check their references. Let us repeat: Check their references—this is very important. Here are some questions you can ask when doing a referral check.

For more info, reach out to us at: www.cabinvestments.com, 708-316-0545, or mikeandmarisa@theseniorhousingbook.com.

Referral Check Questions

When Did This Contractor Perform Work at Your Home?

Was it three weeks ago or three years ago? If it is a recent referral, that is even better.

What Work Did This Contractor Do for You and How Did You Like the Job?

Make sure the work you need done is something they have completed in the past. Contractors will often say that they do certain work, but it is not really their specialty.

Would You Recommend This Contractor to Someone Else?

If you would not recommend the contractor to someone else, that contractor is probably not the right person for you.

Getting Multiple Bids

It is good to have options. Although price is important, other factors such as reputation, quality, and speed to complete the job are also important. We recommend getting at least three bids before picking a contractor and starting work.

What to Get Done First

This is going to depend a lot on the nature of the situation. When a senior starts losing their mobility, the first items on the list are modifications to the bathroom and adding handrails in the home, while converting the bathtub to a walk-in shower is another popular choice.

Steps

Steps and any sort of elevation changes can be extremely dangerous to seniors with mobility challenges. In this regard, converting a series of steps into a ramp and adding handrails can help.

Lighting

A lot of accidents happen in the evening when people are moving around in no or low lighting. Increase the lighting in your home, whether by adding a new lighting fixture or using removable touch lighting. Plug-in nightlights can also help. You could also consider setting the lights on a timer, based upon the time of day, so that when night falls, the lighting automatically comes on.

Security

It is no secret that senior citizens can be targets for thugs and thieves, and therefore adding a security system can keep the bad guys away. A wearable panic button is another deterrent, which can provide notification to emergency personnel if the wearer has a fall. You can also purchase stand-alone systems to request help if there is an accident in the home.

Outdoor lighting with motion sensors adds another layer to your home security. Max installed a front door camera for his grandmother that linked up to her TV. If someone came to the door, it took her about two minutes to make the walk there. The camera therefore provided her with peace of mind.

A Scooter or Walker

Even if you do not need to use a mobility aid all the time, they can really help if you need to take a break. There are some walkers that have a seat on them in order to allow you to rest on long-distance treks. Max's grandmother would use her walker and sit down on it while she was cooking—it was her mobile chair. Make sure to get a walker with a basket on the front to help carry mail or remotes.

The rubber stoppers on the bottom of walkers will wear out, so be ready to get your Swiss army knife out and have an endless supply of tennis balls.

Electric scooters can be used both outside and inside the home. Most are narrow enough to get around your home without causing damage. They are heavy, so plan accordingly; however, lighter models are available.

Electric scooters can be pricey, but how much would it be worth to you to be able to go to the zoo with your grandkids and chase them around? Max chose the four-wheel model for his grandmother because of its increased stability.

Open Lines of Communication

Max's grandmother had been falling down in her home but had not told her family. She was afraid that she would become a burden if they knew. Maybe she was also worried about being sent to an assisted living center—she was very wary of such places. There was even a time that she fell down and could not get up for almost 24 hours.

Let your senior family member know that if they fall down or get in trouble, you are there to help them. Max assured his grandmother that she had helped him during the first 15 years of his life, so he was going to help her for as many years as she had left on this planet.

Max has often stated that he would have traded all the money in his bank account to get one more day with her. You hear about people paying

$10 million to go into outer space. If he had $10 million and that could buy him one more hour with his grandmother, he would pay it instantly.

Step 3 – Bringing in Help

There are two kinds of care that seniors at different stages in their lives could possibly need if they stay in their home: skilled medical care and personal care.

Medical care is when a trained medical professional comes into the home and helps with medical needs, such as providing medicine or therapy.

Personal care might include taking someone to doctor's appointments, shopping, food preparation, bathing, and helping with eating, dressing, or doing the laundry.

For more info, reach out to us at: www.cabinvestments.com, 708-316-0545, or mikeandmarisa@theseniorhousingbook.com.

There are many different kinds of agencies that provide these types of care. In fact, we could write a whole book on this subject. Below are some questions you can ask when you are interviewing a home care agency:

- *What services do you provide?*

- *How long have you been providing these services?*

- *Are you licensed by the state?*

- *Do you perform background checks on your staff?*

- *How will you communicate with my family members if needed?*

- *Are your caregivers available 24 hours a day?*

Finding Caregivers

Referrals from people you know, like, and trust are a great place to start. A local church is a good place, too. Even if you find a good person or agency from a credible source, you will still want to get them checked out.

Perform a referral check before you bring anyone into your home, and ask for a copy of their proof of insurance. It is important for your whole team to interview them. Seniors can be trusting people. Have other people on your advisory team present in order to ensure that there are no red flags.

Step 4 – Are They Coming Back?

What happens if your senior has left their home due to a medical issue and moving back is no longer an option?

If you have been maintaining the home for the senior to move back into and now they are no longer going to do so, do they still want to keep the home? As stated in the previous chapter, if things change and you do decide you want to sell your home, the better condition the home is in, the more you are going to get for it.

If your senior needs minor medical attention or was just admitted to the hospital, do not put the home on the market the next day. After three to six months of them being away from home, and for sure by the one-year mark, your team will usually have a pretty good sense of what is going to happen with your loved one and what needs to happen to the home.

Passing the Home Down to Another

If your goal is to pass the home down to another family member, there are two different times that this can happen:

1. While the senior homeowner is still alive

2. When the senior homeowner has passed away

If the House Has to Change Hands Sooner

If your goal is to keep the house in the family and pass it on to somebody else while the senior homeowner is still alive, double-check the laws in your state. Consult an attorney for the best route.

If your senior currently receives government aid for their senior living expenses, you really need to double-check the rules and requirements.

In the next chapters, we will discuss different types of senior housing, including options provided by the government. The government provides aid for seniors that experience financial hardship. If your senior has a property that is paid off, they do not have a financial hardship.

Family members have often asked us if they can transfer a home into someone else's name with the intent of sheltering the home from their senior's personal balance sheet.

Does that sound legal or ethical to you? It does not sound legal or ethical to us—it sounds illegal and unethical. Our advice is to consult an attorney before transferring real estate into someone else's name or before any real estate transaction.

Also, when planning to transfer property to a family member, consult an accountant to see if there are any tax implications. In some states, customers may use a quitclaim deed to pass real estate to a family member when there is no financial transaction involved. Consult your legal team.

For more info, reach out to us at: www.cabinvestments.com, 708-316-0545, or mikeandmarisa@theseniorhousingbook.com.

Things That Can Go Wrong

The biggest thing that can go wrong is if your senior's physical condition rapidly worsens—watch out for that. Sometimes, the senior does not want to let on that things are not going well because losing their independence is a big deal.

Create an environment where the senior can tell the members of the team what is really going on. Trust but verify. If there is a vacant home, keep it under close watch. If there is a relative that starts getting unruly, have all of your legal documents ready.

When Is the Right Time for a Decision?

When it comes to keeping your home, plan out three or four of the most common scenarios with your team. For each scenario, pick some ideal outcomes and write them down in your Senior Planning Guide.

When something starts to change, you will have at least 90% of the decisions planned out, and then you and the team can figure out the remaining 10%.

An Example Plan

I want to live in my home for as long as possible. I have budgeted $300 a month for home maintenance. When I need personal or medical care for more than eight hours a day, I want to move to a facility where somebody can attend to me and I can get access to more advanced care.

My first preference would be to live with a family member, as long as I am not a burden to them. If no one wants to take me into their home, I want to move into a senior facility that is the least restrictive environment possible.

If it does not look like I can move back into my home or if my condition does not improve after six months of living in a senior facility, I would like my oldest daughter to sell my home and put the money into an account that can be used to pay for my living expenses.

After I pass on, I want my oldest daughter to execute the trust with a specific attorney and follow the guidelines therein.

This is an example of what your Senior Housing Plan can look like.

How We Can Help?

It has been said that an ounce of prevention is worth a pound of cure. We have a large database of contractors we know, like, and trust. If you reach out to us at, we will refer someone to you. We also have professional service providers we can refer to you.

Share this book with your family members, and if you do decide to sell your home, give us a call and we can review your options.

The Goal

The goal of this chapter has been to give you some ideas about how to keep your home and some things to look out for in the process. In the next chapter, we will discuss some of the choices in senior housing if you decide that your current home is not meeting all of your needs.

Chapter 5: Senior Housing Choices

Right Idea, Wrong Plan

Margo never told her adult children, James and Mary, that she had been falling at home. When James took his mom to the doctor, the doctor noticed that there were marks on Margo's shoulder and hip.

Margo told the doctor that she had scraped up against a shrub and bumped into the wall, but the doctor could tell that something was not quite right. After a short period of time, Margo came clean.

Her family worked on a Senior Housing Plan, wherein Margo could get more care and feel more secure. Although Margo was having some mobility issues, she was doing great otherwise. She had been taking her medicine, cooking for herself, and even doing her own chores.

James and the family did not have a good understanding of all the different choices in senior housing. They put Margo in a facility that had a lot of services, even though most of them were not really necessary for her. The new assisted living center took care of her medicine, food preparation, and laundry, amongst other activities.

Margo was now paying almost three times what she could have been paying if she was in a less restrictive facility. The facility was great, but the level of care was too high for Margo's needs, and the huge monthly bill created a financial strain on the family.

Use It or Lose It

An unexpected side effect of Margo's new facility and service offerings was that she stopped doing things for herself. She became more and more dependent on the facility as the days progressed, and she lost her independence little by little in the process.

Chapter Goal

The goal of this chapter is to outline some of the major senior housing choices out there (new choices are becoming available all the time) and to list the pros and cons of each facility.

This chapter will not be able to cover all the available choices. However, the major categories that are covered should give you and your team an idea of what to expect as you start building out your Senior Housing Plan.

A lot of customers are not sure whether to sell or keep their house (see previous chapters) until they have understood what their local options are.

For more info, reach out to us at: www.cabinvestments.com, 708-316-0545, or mikeandmarisa@theseniorhousingbook.com.

Right Facility at the Right Time

How do you pick a senior living facility before you need to be in one?

What will it take for you and your family to be happy with a senior housing facility?

Will this facility be able to grow with you if you end up needing more care, or will you have to move to a different facility?

These are some of the questions that we are going to address in this chapter. When it comes to senior housing, there is a wide range of options, services, and prices. Make sure that you understand what is included and what is not (extras) when you are looking for a new residence. Think about what kind of care you need now but also what kind of care you may need in the future.

Hopefully, you are looking at senior living facilities before you need to be in one. If there has been a recent and sudden health change, you may not have the luxury of time.

Three Levels of Care

1. *Independent* – Seniors are fully or mostly independent.

2. *Assisted* – Personal care assistance.

3. *Nursing* – Skilled medical care.

Making Your Plan

If you are currently independent, figure out what will be important to you in a new facility and plan out a couple of choices for each of the categories above.

Having some facilities already narrowed down will give you and your family peace of mind in case a sudden change happens. If there has been a recent sudden change, use the information and checklists in this chapter to identify what level of care you need and start your search today.

Recent Events

So, you made the decision to sell your home once you found a good senior housing facility. What led to this decision?

Downsizing

The house in which you raised your family and currently live in may not fit your current needs anymore. If only one or two seniors live in a house designed to fit a large family, that home may be too much to handle.

We often buy houses from customers who, due to mobility issues, have not been upstairs in months or even years. Even if you can afford the maintenance and upkeep on a bigger home, you may decide living in it is not worth the trouble.

Medical Change

Has there been a recent medical change? Are you losing your mobility or memory? Do need more medical care now than you can manage by yourself? Even if you could live on your own, would you feel better and safer if someone could keep an eye on you?

For more info, reach out to us at: www.cabinvestments.com, 708-316-0545, or mikeandmarisa@theseniorhousingbook.com.

Timeline

Hopefully, you are in planning mode, and there has not been a situation or reason to move out yet. All being well, you have plenty of time to evaluate your options. If that is not the case, and you are in fast-track mode, do not hesitate. Read through this chapter, and start finding a facility today.

Benefits of Solving Early

There are many benefits to planning your senior housing early.

Vacancy

The best cost-to-value facilities in our area fill up quickly and can be hard to get into. A customer called one of our offices saying that she needed us to buy her home that day because she had found out that an apartment had opened up in a facility she really liked. She had been on the waiting list for over 12 months.

The facility required her to put a deposit down and make a decision quickly because they had a waiting list. If you wait until the last minute to make a senior housing choice, the only places left might be the really expensive ones or those you do not want to live in.

Supply and Demand

Senior housing is typically expensive. High-quality, inexpensive places can fill fast, so you want to have these places on your shortlist and figure out how far in advance you need to reserve a spot.

In many parts of the country, it seems like someone is building a new senior housing facility all the time. In many cities, there is more supply than demand, but as more seniors reach retirement age and new seniors move into those areas, that could shift.

Preparation So Far

The internet is a blessing and a curse. Before the internet, you had the library, newspapers, TV, and other people to choose from if you wanted information. There were no online reviews or referral services (or even websites). At present, all this information at our fingertips can create more confusion than clarity.

Information Overload

Do blogs, online reviews, websites, and online advertisements create clarity or information overload? Is all the information online about senior housing true or objective? When someone is posting an online article about senior housing, is the information a fact or a clever sales letter? At his church, a pastor advised that "information is NOT the same thing as wisdom."

Some customers start their research online, and that is not a bad choice. They have read a bunch of top-five articles and have looked at reviews and websites, and they are more confused than before after all this research and are no closer to making a senior housing decision.

Pricing is an area that is rarely disclosed online or even over the phone. Each type of facility is unique in its own way, so it is very difficult to compare one facility to another.

By the end of this chapter, we hope that you will be able to map out what is important to you, know how to locate facilities, and be able to choose the right one. In the next chapter, we will give you information about the costs at the different facilities.

For more info, reach out to us at: www.cabinvestments.com, 708-316-0545, or mikeandmarisa@theseniorhousingbook.com.

Picture Perfect

Imagine having a Senior Housing Plan prepared in advance that you can hand to a family member if needed. This plan would break down the three major categories of senior living facilities and have one or two places already screened and selected.

Instead of being in a rush, you had ample time to pick the senior housing facility that has the right mix of values, staff excellence, service, and price.

Choices

1. Independent Living

2. Assisted Living

3. Nursing Care

In the following sections, we are going to outline some of the most popular senior housing choices and do our best to objectively give you the pros and cons of each choice.

Independent Living

Age-Restricted Communities

Age-restricted communities can be apartments, single-family homes, garden homes, and even townhouses. These communities have a "connected" feel and attract seniors that want to have access to activities ranging from arts and crafts and bingo to the gym and a swimming pool.

Some facilities with higher-end amenities may add golf or tennis.

This type of facility is normally geared towards independent seniors who could live on their own, in their own houses, but really want to socialize with other people their age. They are also looking for less home and yard maintenance than if they lived on their own.

Most independent living age-restricted communities do not allow people under 55 years old to live there, so if your daughter lives with you right now and you are thinking about moving to an age-restricted community, you need to check with that community to make sure that this would be possible.

One of our partner companies bought a home from a couple who were moving to a 55+ community. They were going to live in an apartment, work their normal jobs, and go camping in their towable camper on weekends and holidays. They had a beautiful home but wanted a place that required less maintenance.

Senior Apartments, Townhouses, and Garden Homes

These types of senior housing are similar to the previous option but usually have fewer amenities and are cheaper. They are a great option for folks that are downsizing but still want privacy.

Some of these senior communities have a percentage of units available to lower-income seniors that qualify. In addition, these communities can have a gated entrance and ADA-compliant units. They can be a great opportunity for someone who does not need as much socialization as in a fancier community but still wants to live in a community of seniors.

For more info, reach out to us at: www.cabinvestments.com, 708-316-0545, or mikeandmarisa@theseniorhousingbook.com.

Move In with a Family Member

This is becoming a popular choice for many reasons, one of which is finance. Although there is competition among senior housing providers, most senior housing is more expensive than a basic home mortgage.

All senior housing is more expensive than living with a family member. If something does not go according to plan or there is no plan, living with a family member can be one of your only options.

Living with family can be a good or bad idea, depending on the family dynamics. Do not plan on becoming your family's best friend if there was already a strained relationship and now you have to move in with them. On the other hand, if your relationship is really great, moving in may not be a burden at all.

Some customers have their parent(s) move in for health and safety reasons, and the grandparent(s) can be at home when the grandkids come back from school. As a former math teacher, Max recalls that some of his best students had grandparents living with them. They would meet them at home after school, hold them accountable for their schoolwork, and tutor them.

In order to make this arrangement work, everyone needs to be on the same page, which goes back to planning. We have met families where the husband feels great about their parent moving in but the wife or grandkids do not.

Start this conversation today (if you have not done so already). If my kids do not want to take me in, I would rather find out now—while I still have time to create a plan B—rather than have them resent me when my physical condition is poor.

Ask your wife or family this simple question: "If my mom needs to leave her home, can she move in with us? Why or why not?"

If you are a senior and you are thinking about moving in with one of your kids or family members, ask them what they think about the idea. The best way to get a true answer from someone is to let them know that it is a "yes" or "no" question and that whatever answer they give is acceptable—you just want to know how they truly feel.

If you decide to move into a family member's home, find out what their house rules are. Get some space and privacy for yourself. Having your own room or quiet place to be alone will help everyone. Set boundaries ahead of time, e.g., "After 7 pm, I really just need some time by myself to think and pray."

A few years back, a senior couple sold their house, and their adult son also sold his house. They decided to pool their resources and bought some land with two houses, one for each family.

If the porch light was on, that meant they were accepting visitors (grandkids and other family members). If the porch light was off, they needed alone time. That sounds like it could be fun if you get along with your family.

Renting a Room to Live in or Renting Out a Room in Your House

You can keep your home and rent out a room. Many have lived with seniors and helped them around the house in exchange for free or reduced rent.

Some are a little skeptical of this arrangement, maybe because of the numerous horror stories that have aired on the news. Having a stranger living in your home may not sound like a great idea. However, if you want to explore this further, here are some things to look out for.

You do not want just anyone living in your house—it has to be the right person. Safety is the primary concern. If you go to live in a house with either a group of seniors or an adult that rents out a room, the same thing applies. You must be very careful any time you live with strangers.

We do not recommend either one of these options unless you really know the person, and even then you want to get a full background check and always trust your instincts. We have heard of more of these situations turning out bad than good.

Now, if there is a situation where you have three people from church who have been best friends for 30 years, and they are all widows in their 80s, that might work. However, you still need your own space and to set ground rules for the home.

Set up personal boundaries. It is a lot easier to be friends with somebody when you see them at church or hang out with each other for two or three hours at a time than to actually live with them.

For more info, reach out to us at: www.cabinvestments.com, 708-316-0545, or mikeandmarisa@theseniorhousingbook.com.

Assisted Living

Assisted Living – Corporate Location

Assisted living facilities can give you access to a large range of services, from help with basic personal care, such as getting dressed, taking medicine, and bathing, to more advanced assistance. Assisted living facilities can feel like living in a big house or hotel, and most facilities are fully furnished.

Some facilities have a more independent, apartment-style wing with a different area that focuses more on hands-on care. Services at these facilities can include meals, daily activities, transportation, and security.

If a senior is starting to have memory problems but can still live independently, they may be able to live in an assisted living facility. If the senior needs more advanced memory services, those are handled in a special care unit that normally comes under the umbrella of skilled nursing care.[3]

You can choose from national brands or local non-chain facilities. Look at each location on a facility-by-facility basis before making your selection. Your decision will come down to the mix of people living and working there and the price for the value that you are getting. A great management team is a must-have.

Questions to Consider

How do the managers connect with the staff and residents?

How long has the management team been in place?

---

[3] Source: "Residential Care, Such as Assisted Living, Memory Care, & Nursing Homes for Persons with Dementia," *Dementia Care Central*, 19 September 2018. Retrieved from www.dementiacarecentral.com/memory-care-vs-assisted-living/

Is it a for profit or non-profit facility?

How do the workers interact with the residents and with each other?

Most of the facilities we visit are full of managers and workers that want to be there.

For more info, reach out to us at www.cabinvestments.com, 708-316-0545, or mikeandmarisa@theseniorhousingbook.com.

Residential Assisted Living Facilities

These assisted living facilities are converted single-family houses in a neighborhood or small buildings that have been built to house a small group of seniors. Most facilities have between six and 18 seniors per property. These facilities offer some of the same services as the larger assisted living facilities.

At the facilities we have been to, we have noticed a close-knit community feel. One of our customers, who moved into a residential assisted living facility, was able to stay in a similar neighborhood to where she had lived before. She told us that her favorite aspects of the facility were the friendships with the residents and the large back porch and yard. Max's great aunt, a retired nurse who never married, also had a good experience in one of these properties.

Residents who are drawn to these properties like the idea of being in a home, getting to share a meal with a small group of people, getting to go into the backyard, and feeling like they are still in their old homes. The downside is that if two or three other residents really get on your nerves, it is hard to escape from them as you could in a larger facility.

Typically, there is a staff member that arrives in the morning and someone who stays in the evening and overnight. Most places also have a nurse who is on call if needed. Many of these facilities have meal services with a chef that cooks for the guests. Rooms could be private or shared with another senior.

The management team could include someone with a real estate background who has learned how to serve seniors or individuals who have worked for larger facilities and want to be at a smaller location. We have had many clients that have moved into these types of homes with great success.

Memory Care

Memory care facilities or special care units (SPU) are specifically for patients with Alzheimer's or other forms of dementia. These units are specially designed to protect patients from getting lost. They have treatment options available to address behavioral needs, since Alzheimer's and other forms of dementia evolve with each stage.[4]

The staff at these types of facilities are skilled at identifying changes in these stages and adjusting the patient's treatment plan accordingly. Patients are encouraged to live as independently as possible.

The benefits of these facilities include fewer patient falls, less hospital visits, and a consistent administering of medicine, as opposed to a resident insisting on living in their own home in a confused state.

Although these facilities can be in a separate area of an assisted living facility, the residents interact with other community members and are not isolated.

Nursing Care

Nursing Homes

Skilled nursing facilities (SNF) are facilities for individuals that require skilled nursing (medical)

---

[4] Source: Residential Care, Such as Assisted Living, Memory Care, & Nursing Homes for Persons with Dementia," *Dementia Care Central*, 19 September 2018. Retrieved from www.dementiacarecentral.com/memory-care-vs-assisted-living/

care. As the name implies, these facilities are staffed by nurses. In this regard, care is provided by registered nurses (RNs), licensed practical nurses, (LPNs), and licensed vocational nurses (LVNs).[5]

These professionals are available 24 hours a day, and care at these facilities can include:

- Personal care (e.g., housekeeping, laundry, meals, and bathing)

- Monitoring medical signs

- Management of a patient's care plan

- Observing a patient's conditions

- Tube feedings

- Rehabilitation services

- Therapeutic exercises or activities

- Dental services

- Recreational activities.

Some treatments are provided by skilled staff and some are provided by other specialists, such as occupational therapists and speech therapists,

---

[5] Source: "Aging & Health A to Z." *Health in Aging*. Retrieved from www.healthinaging.org/aging-and-health-a-toz/topic:nursing-homes/

who come into the facility to treat patients but are not permanent staff members.[6]

Not every nursing home provides the same services, so make sure you know what they offer and what they do not. Below are some examples of the specialized care that may be available at some facilities but not at all:

- Rehabilitative therapy

- Dialysis

- Working with Alzheimer's and dementia patients

- IV drug therapy.

CCRC (Continuing Care Retirement Communities)

This type of community is a hybrid since it can fit into all three categories. To be classified as a CCRC (life-plan community), a community must offer independent living, assisted living, and skilled nursing care all in the same facility or campus.

If you are a senior, you have to move in when you are healthy and are currently living independently. Communities can consist of

---

[6] Source: Bernal, N. "Skilled Nursing Care: Fact vs. Myth," *Care Conversations*, 29 October 2014. Retrieved from careconversations.org/skilled-nursing-care-fact-vs-myth

houses, townhouses, or apartments, while the amenities available can be at the resort level, frequently including golf, tennis, and other higher-end amenities.[7]

CCRCs generally have an ownership option, which we will discuss more in the next chapter. If your budget is high, you are looking for a resort-style retirement, and you like the idea of services as you need them without forcing you to move out, look into a CCRC.[8]

3 Steps to Finding Your Ideal Facility

Hopefully, this framework and all the knowledge from the previous chapters will get you and your team into the right mindset to tackle this opportunity.

1. Needs and wants

2. Identify and interview

3. Decision

---

[7] Source: "CCRC vs Rental Retirement Community | MyLifeSite Blog," *MyLifeSite*, 2 July 2018. Retrieved from www.mylifesite.net/blog/post/ccrc-vs-rental-retirement-community-what-are-the-differences/

[8] Source: "From Family Caregiving to Retirement Communities," *AARP*. Retrieved from www.aarp.org/caregiving/basics/info-2017/continuing-care-retirement-communities.html

Needs and Wants

You need to identify your current needs, forecast your possible future needs, and identify your wants or "wish list." Price is important, but do not let it be the sole determining factor in your decision.

I have had multiple customers who started calling up local facilities and asking them how much they charge. Most of the facilities told them, "It depends on what you want or need."

Pricing is more complicated than booking a hotel room. Come up with your needs, preferences, and a basic idea of your budget—then see where the process leads you. Answer each one of these following questions with your team.

For more info, reach out to us at: www.cabinvestments.com, 708-316-0545, or mikeandmarisa@theseniorhousingbook.com.

Setting Up Your Plan Checklist

Your Plan

❑ Are there any current problems or challenges you are facing?

❑ What is the single biggest problem you are trying to solve?

❑ How soon do you expect to move into a senior housing facility?

❑ What geographical location do you want to live in?

❑ Do you have a specific housing need right now? If so, what is it (i.e., independent, assisted, nursing, specialty)?

❑ What has prompted you to start this search?

❑ Where do you currently live?

❑ How long will it take to sell your home and/or move?

❑ Who are the members of your advisory team (e.g., spouse, children, family members, pastor, medical team, or professionals)?

❏ Is your advisory team part of your planning process?

❏ If price were no object, where would you want to live?

❏ What type of environment do you want to live in (e.g., private, community, social, private room, shared room, private house, or first floor)?

❏ What amenities would you like to have available (e.g., entertainment, recreation, food, pool, classes, and transportation)?

❏ What types of personal care services do you need now or want to be available (e.g., dressing, mobility help, laundry, bathing, and food)?

❏ What type of medical care services do you need now or want to be available (e.g., treatments, specialty care, medicine, and diabetes care)?

Your Team

❑ Do you have the following professionals on your team yet? If so, list them below:

  ❑ Attorney

  ❑ Financial advisor

  ❑ CPA

  ❑ Medical doctor

  ❑ Family members and other advisors

❑ Are there any other needs or wants you have that are important to you but have not been mentioned yet?

❑ What is important to the members of your advisory team? Ask them if you have not already. For example, "I am creating a Senior Housing Plan that I expect to begin following (fill in the date, e.g., next month, next year, or in ten years). What is important to you?"

❑ Ask your advisory team, "Is there anything else you want me to consider as I am creating my plan"?

Your Closest Advisor

- ❏ Do you have any concerns regarding my health, safety, and overall happiness?

- ❏ What problems or challenges are you facing as my top advisor?

- ❏ Is moving in with you or anyone else in our family an option?

Other Planning Questions

- ❏ Are you married?

- ❏ Do you currently live with anyone else?

- ❏ If you move, where is your current house partner (e.g., friend, family, or spouse) going to live?

- ❏ If your spouse were to die before you, would you want to stay in your current home?

- ❏ Would you prefer to move into a facility that has all the care options available—from independent to nursing—or would you be fine moving to a new facility if you needed more care?

- ❏ Do you want to be close to a church?

❏ Is there a friend or family member you want to live close to?

❏ If you are thinking about moving across the city, state, or country, will you need to find a new doctor or other professionals?

❏ If you are moving into a furnished facility, what is the plan for your current furniture and personal belongings?

❏ If you plan to give items from your home away to family members, have you let your family members know?

❏ Will you get input from your family members before you give them any of your personal belongings?

❏ When you give a family member or friend your personal belongings, are they theirs to keep or are you just letting them store them for you?

❏ Will you need to rent a storage facility? If so, where?

❏ How will you know when it is time to make a decision?

Your Budget

- ❏ Do you use a monthly budget?

- ❏ What monthly budget amount can you afford for senior housing and care expenses?

- ❏ What financial sources are available to pay for senior housing?

- ❏ If you do not need senior housing right now, have you inquired about long-term care insurance?

- ❏ Do you expect family members to help pay for your housing? If so, how much do they plan to contribute?

- ❏ If you plan to sell your home, how much do you expect to receive?

Identify and Interview

Once you map out what is important to you and your team, and you have a basic idea and budget of what you want and need, start identifying and interviewing facilities. You can find facilities online, from print media, referrals from friends, or by contacting local or national referral services.

Answer the questions below at each step of the process. After you narrow down your choices, you should plan to visit a minimum of three to four facilities of each type of care you are planning for. Carry a checklist for each facility so that you can evaluate and compare them at the end.

For more info, reach out to us at www.cabinvestments.com, 708-316-0545, or mikeandmarisa@theseniorhousingbook.com.

Before You Call (Identify)

❏ How did I find out about this facility?

❏ How many of my needs does this facility meet?

❏ How many of my wants does this facility meet?

❏ Does this facility have the level of care I may need in the future?

❏ What do the online reviews say about this facility? (See Google, Facebook, and the Better Business Bureau).

Call the Facility (Phone Interview)

❏ Do you have any openings at your facility?

❏ What services do you provide?

❏ Do you perform background checks on your staff? What about the residents?

❏ Is your facility accredited? If so, with who?

❏ How much should I budget if I move into your facility (not an exact number, just a range)?

❏ If I become a resident, how often do rates change?

❏ What is the best way I can get more information about your facility?

❏ When can I take a tour of the facility and learn more?

Questions for the Tour (In-Person Interview)

❏ Ask your tour person how long they have worked there and what their main focus is?

❏ Who is the current manager or director? How long have they been there?

❏ What services are not offered here?

❏ What do you like about working here?

❏ What would you change about the facility if you could?

❏ Ask if you can speak to any other employees and residents about their experience at the facility

❏ How do you communicate with family members?

❏ When are the visiting hours?

❏ Do they have any referrals of current residents or past residents/family members that you can contact?

❏ Is this a for profit or non-profit facility? If you have experience with each one, what differences do you see in these?

❏ If I were to move in today and order certain services, what would my price be?

❏ How often do rates change for residents?

❏ How often do rates change for the general public who are not currently residents?

❏ How many openings do you have right now?

❏ Is the rate open to negotiation? If so, under what circumstances?

❏ What is the application process? How long does it take?

❑ Are there any questions I should have asked that I did not?

❑ How long can we take to make a decision?

Decision

After your interviews and tours, it is time to sit down with your team and narrow the list down to your top two choices. If you need to move quickly, call your top facility and start the application process. If your top facility is not available when you need it, you can choose the alternative.

If moving into a senior housing facility is not in the immediate future, having a couple of choices in each of the three areas already narrowed down will drastically cut down on the time it takes to pick the search back up when making a choice becomes urgent.

Things That Can Go Wrong

1. The facility you want is full.

2. Picking the wrong level of care.

3. Not properly budgeting (if at all).

If the facility you want is fully booked, get on the waiting list. If you are planning ahead, you can get on the waiting list ahead of time so that when you are ready to move in 6 or 12 months, there should be an opening. If you are really serious about moving in to a certain facility, putting down a small deposit may be part of the process.

The wrong level of care can be an expensive mistake. All of the extra services you get can look easy on the pocket by themselves, but together they can be a budget buster—you want to live somewhere you can afford.

Just like you check your monthly bank statements for charges you are not expecting, if cost is a concern, make sure that you are only receiving the services you really need.

You do not want to get three or six months into living at a new facility and find out you cannot afford to live there any longer. Getting an accurate estimate of all costs and possible increases before you move in will help you mitigate this risk.

You have to set your monthly budget and plan for all your expenses, not just for your senior housing. The sooner you start understanding the costs of senior living and how you will be able to save and budget for it, the more successful you will be.

At the time of writing this book, we do not own any senior living facilities, but we have looked at the financial statements of different assisted living facilities as a possible investor. These facilities charge a lot because they have very large expenses—it costs a lot of money to have ADA buildings, staff, meals, insurance, etc.

Build out your plan and expect to pay more than you have ever paid for housing and other services. In the next chapter, we will review some costs, so between this book and the facility tours you will go on, you will have the information you need to get your budget ready.

Next Steps

The decision to plan is yours. The time to begin the plan is today. The decision to move really depends on what you or your team agrees on. Hopefully, you have been equipped with some new ideas and information that will help. We hope that the checklists in this book will help with organizing your process so that you can get results faster.

For more info, reach out to us at: www.cabinvestments.com, 708-316-0545, or mikeandmarisa@theseniorhousingbook.com.

The Goal

The goal of this chapter has been to go over some of the most popular senior housing choices and facilitate a discussion between you and your senior housing team.

If you have gone through all the questions and steps in this chapter, then you are more knowledgeable about senior housing than 99% of your peers. If you know a senior or family member of a senior that could also use this information, reach out to us at, so that we can get this book into their hands.

Feel free to share this book with your community groups, friends, and churches. We have a limited number of free workshops that we can put on each month. If your church or community would like us to speak, reach out to us to set something up.

Home To Home

Chapter 6: The Cost of Senior Housing – Paying The Bills

A man put his dad into a nursing home after he had sold his parent's house. The nursing home was not cheap—$7,200 a month. The dad lived there for five years, at the end of which the money from the house was all gone.

What did the family do? They moved the dad in with family members and took turns taking care of him.

When will your money run out? How much do you have each month for senior housing, and will it be enough? Hopefully, you will be able to take some nuggets away from this chapter that will help you get better prepared.

Costs and Affordability

This is the question everyone wants to know, but it is the hardest to answer precisely. Why? Because there are so many variables. Our goal for this chapter is to share some average numbers with you that our customers are seeing in many parts of the country at the time of publishing this book. Such numbers will give you a starting point, and by using the tools in the previous chapter, you will be able to get the exact numbers for your area.

Good luck!

Independent Care

Our customers have told us that they pay between $1,000 a month (for a small gated apartment with few amenities) to over $4,000 a month (for a higher-end planned community). Most places with a large list of amenities and services will have a base rate in the $2,000 to $3,000 a month range and then add other services or memberships on top of that if desired.[9]

Keep in mind that there are deals to be found in any market. If you are flexible with regard to location and amenities, friend referrals, extensive searching, and local referral agencies can help cut the amounts above in half.

Remember from Chapter 4 that living in your existing home is not free. Time is the only resource you cannot get more of. Do you want to spend your precious time, the last of your time on this earth, mowing your yard and trimming your trees to save money? If you have always thought that way, it will be a hard mindset to shift, but it is never too late.

If you still have a mortgage on your house, remember that the amount you have in the budget, along with taxes and maintenance from your current home, will now go towards your new housing. When you factor that in, a facility in the price range above may not be that much more than what you are currently paying.

---

[9] Source: "Independent Living Community Price Ranges and Costs," *Brookdale Senior Living Solutions*. Retrieved from www.brookdale.com/en/where-to-begin/financialconsiderations/independent-living-price-range.html

Another benefit is that most independent living facilities have already been retrofitted to help people with mobility issues. If you planned to pay $5,000 or $10,000 on your current home in order to make some changes to it, you can now apply that amount to your new facility (which already has done that for you). How convenient!

Assisted Living Facilities

According to the Genworth Financial Cost of Care Survey released in April by Genworth Financial Inc. of Richmond, the national median monthly rate for a one-bedroom unit in an assisted living facility is $4,000.[10]

According to a report by Acclaro Growth Partners, the average stay in an assisted living facility is 29 months.

So, if you take the $4,000 and multiply it by 29 months, that is over $100,000—the national average. There are facilities in our market that are far from fancy and are much higher than that. Who is going to pay for that?

---

[10] Source: "Cost of Care," The 2018 Cost of Care Report, *Genworth*. Retrieved from www.genworth.com/aging-and-you/ finances/cost-of-care.html

For more info, reach out to us at: www.cabinvestments.com, 708-316-0545, or mikeandmarisa@theseniorhousingbook.com.

Nursing Care Facilities

According to the American Health Care Association (*www.ahcancal.org*), 59% of assisted living residents will eventually move to a skilled nursing facility. The average stay in a nursing home is one to three years.[11]

In many parts of the country, nursing home prices can be $7,000 a month and higher. If you put all these costs together—and consider that, on average, you are looking at about four to five years of some type of long-term care—you can easily come to a total of over $200,000. This estimate does not include any doctor or hospital bills that a senior may incur during that period.

CCRC (Continuing Care Retirement Communities)

Entry fees can range from low- to mid-six figures depending on your location. These entry

---

[11] Source: "So I'll Probably Need Long-Term Care, But for How Long? *MyLifeSite*, 28 June 2018. Retrieved from www.mylifesite. net/blog/post/so-ill-probably-need-long-term-care-but-for-how-long/

fees allow you to live in a home or condo in the planned community. Monthly charges range from $2,000 to more than $4000 a month.[12]

These facilities have contracts called Life Care or Type A that will cover all your care at the facility, even if your level of care goes up. Since the facility is taking on more risk, you are required to provide a larger down payment.

Type B contracts allow you to pay for discounted care when you need it, and they do not require as much of a down payment. If your long-term care policy will cover your extra care costs, you can elect a Type C fee for a service contract that will charge you the going rate when care is needed.

A declining portion of the entry fee is refunded if the resident dies within a few years of moving in. Some people pay the entrance fee of the CCRC with the proceeds from the sale of their home. If you are a couple moving to a CCRC, expect to pay between $200,000 and $300,000,

---

[12] Source: Fried, C. "Continuing Care Retirement Community: Can You Afford It?" *Time*, 22 December 2016. Retrieved from time.com/money/4579934/continuing-care-retirement-communities-cost/

plus a monthly charge of around $2,000 per resident.[13]

The majority of CCRCs are run by non-profits and many have a religious affiliation.

Timeline

Do not move into a facility unless you understand all the costs involved and what your budget is. Once you have these mapped out, you can figure out the next step based on your plan. If your budget is on the lower side, you will want to start planning even sooner because great places at budget prices fill up faster in most markets.

Look for a place that has a good value-to-cost ratio. You may not get everything on your wish list, so be willing to make compromises if you have to on the items that are not as important to you.

If you have long-term care insurance and a significant nest egg saved up, pick your dream location. Enjoy your senior housing experience!

---

[13] Source: Fried, C. "Continuing Care Retirement Community: Can You Afford It?" *Time*, 22 December 2016. Retrieved from time.com/money/4579934/continuing-care-retirement-communities-cost/

It Never Hurts to Ask

You can negotiate the rates at some facilities. You can receive move-in specials and some services added at a discount. During your working career, you wanted to get paid for your work—so do senior living facilities.

There are many things more important than price. Do you want to be in a facility that serves bad food and has very low energy simply to save $500 a month? Most likely, you do not.

Planning

Why is it important to resolve this situation early and get your plan in place? Without a good plan, you can run out of money. You do not want to outlive your budget. This planet rewards planning, so if you have not been a master planner up to this point, now is your chance.

Have you found your perfect facility and created the budget to support it? If so, great job! Do not wait until your life starts winding down. Having your plan in place will give you the comfort and enjoyment to allow you to relax and have as much fun as possible.

For more info, reach out to us at: www.cabinvestments.com, 708-316-0545, or mikeandmarisa@theseniorhousingbook.com.

Paying for Senior Housing

Now that you know the costs, the rest of this chapter will focus on some of the different ways to pay for senior housing. Please consult your financial advisor, attorney, and advisory team to fill in all the details.

Medicare

A large proportion of seniors in America have Medicare as their primary health insurance. Medicare only pays for medical costs but does not pay for the cost of staying in any long-term facility—it does not cover personal care, grooming, eating, transportation, bathing, and other personal care items that are considered non-medical.

Medicare pays for medical care at skilled nursing homes and some types of medical care at assisted living facilities or at home, if it is administered by an independent third party. If you qualify, Medicare will pay for a 20-day-or-less stay in a skilled nursing facility. After 20 days, you have to pay for part of the costs until the 100th day. After 100 days, you pay the full bill.[14]

Medicare Supplemental Insurance

Have you seen the TV ads or received a flyer in the mail for Medicare supplemental insurance? Medicare supplemental insurance is not going to cover long-term nursing home care forever. Medicare supplemental insurance will help fill the gaps from days 20 to 100 in a skilled nursing home facility. At the time of writing, any care that lasts over 100 days will not be paid for by Medicare.[15]

Medicaid

If you have used all your out-of-pocket resources and are out of money, you can attempt to qualify for a state-run Medicaid program. Medicaid is for low-income individuals that have very limited financial assets. If you qualify, Medicaid will pay for nursing care (medical and non-medical expenses) and some home care expenses.

---

[14] Source: "What Is the Current Medicare Coverage for Long-Term Care?" *AARP.* Retrieved from www.aarp.org/health/medicare-qa-tool/current-long-term-nursing-home-coverage/

[15] Source: "Medicare Supplemental Insurance Benefits for Assisted Living & Long-Term Care," *Medicare Supplemental Insurance (Medigap) Benefits for Long-Term Care.* Retrieved from www.payingforseniorcare.com/longtermcare/resources/medigap.html

There are very few assisted living locations available for people on Medicaid. If you only need assisted living care and have very limited financial means, you are probably not going to find a place. In most states, you must have whittled all your assets down to a small amount ($2,000) before Medicaid will kick in.[16]

Long-Term Care Insurance

If you or your senior is younger than 60, it might be time to start looking at a long-term care policy. You can still find policies for clients over 60, but the prices start going up rapidly.

Depending on the policy, long-term care insurance starts kicking in when a senior cannot perform two of the six activities of daily living (ADLs):

1. Eating

2. Going to the bathroom

3. Getting out of a bed or chair

4. Walking

5. Dressing

---

[16] Source: "Nursing Facilities," *Medicaid.gov*. Retrieved from www.medicaid. gov/medicaid/ltss/institutional/nursing/index.html

6. Bathing

Long-term care insurance can cover assisted living, nursing care, Alzheimer's facilities, home modification, home care, adult day care, hospice care, and more. Most policies start covering people on the first day of need. Some policies will also pay for a live-in caregiver. Rates will depend on your health and age, so consult your financial advisor for more details.

Family members with average health who buy into policies at around 60 years of age are paying around $2,000 a year.[17]

For more info, reach out to us at: www.cabinvestments.com, 708-316-0545, or mikeandmarisa@theseniorhousingbook.com.

Reverse Mortgage

A reverse mortgage is something you need to talk about with your financial advisor. It can be complicated and sometimes sounds too good to be true. Instead of taking out a mortgage and making payments to buy a house, a reverse mortgage company will put a lien on a high equity or paid-off house and then pay you.

---

[17] Source: Stark, E. "5 Facts You Should Know About Long-Term Care Insurance," *AARP*, 1 March 2018. Retrieved from www. aarp.org/caregiving/financial-legal/info-2018/long-term-care-insurance-fd.html

A reverse mortgage is a way for you to take equity out of your house without having to sell it. The advantage of this product is that as long as you can keep paying the taxes, insurance, and maintenance, you can stay in the home until you pass away or move. The money that you use from the reverse mortgage will be used during your life and will reduce the amount of your estate.[18]

For some people, this may be the right choice; however, as with any financial instrument, you need to read the fine print and consult your team.

Max's grandmother looked into one of these. After the family reviewed all the documents, they decided not to do it. Her property taxes had almost tripled in a short period of time, but the county was able to defer her taxes until her house was sold.

Max told his grandmother that if she needed to take out a reverse mortgage to stay in her home, her home was probably too expensive for her. If she was not able to defer her property taxes, she would probably have sold the house and either moved in with a family member or moved somewhere cheaper with less maintenance.

---

[18] Source: "14 Important Reverse Mortgage Facts," *New Retirement*, 12 January 2016. Retrieved from www.newretirement.com/ retirement/14-important-reverse-mortgage-facts/

One of the biggest mistakes customers make with reverse mortgages is thinking that they cannot be foreclosed on and that the reverse mortgage company is paying their insurance and their annual property taxes for them.

Many customers have got into property tax trouble and have even been threatened with foreclosure due to delinquent property taxes because the customer thought they were getting paid by the reverse mortgage company—but they were not.

The fine print of some contracts states that not keeping up the maintenance on your home is considered a default against your reverse mortgage, and the lender can foreclose.

On some reverse mortgage agreements, if one of the homeowners dies, the spouse is required to pay back a large amount or the full amount of the loan. That is not the letter you want to get in the mail right after your spouse dies. In addition, interest rates can be pretty high.[19]

---

[19] Source: McKim, J. "More Seniors Are Taking Loans against Their Homes – And It's Costing Them," *The Washington Post*, 25 August 2017. Retrieved from www.washingtonpost.com/business/ economy/more-seniors-are-taking-loans-against-their-homes--and-its-costing-them/2017/08/25/5f154072-883a-11e7-961d-2f373b3977ee_story.html?utm_term=.831aa69 a5b55

Things to Watch Out For

- Prices going up for senior housing

- Rates increasing each year while you are in senior housing

- Fine print

- Understanding the base price and any additional costs

- What Medicare will and will not pay for

- The qualifications for Medicaid.

Reach Out to Us

If you need a referral for anything discussed in this chapter, please give us a call. If you want to create a comprehensive plan with even more detail than we could fit in this book, reach out to us at:

www.cabinvestments.com, 708-316-0545, or mikeandmarisa@theseniorhousingbook.com.

The Goal

The goal of this chapter has been to give you some information on the costs of senior housing and the different ways to pay for it. Senior housing can be a big expense. If you do not have long-term care insurance, there are really only two ways to pay for care: pay out of your pocket, and if that runs all the way down, try to qualify for some services from Medicaid.

When you finish this book, do not put it down and stop there. Start building out your plan. If you do not have a team of people and are nervous about where to start, give us a call and we will help you to figure out the next step.

The following chapter will address some special challenges family members have with the senior planning process. We hope that this next chapter and the questions therein will help your family achieve more clarity.

God Bless!

Chapter 7: Special Challenges for Family Members of Seniors

Getting Older Fast

Every day in America, 10,000 people turn 65.[20]

Who is going to take care of them? Government funds? Personal savings? Family members?

---

[20] Source: Frankel, M. "9 Baby-Boomer Statistics That Will Blow You Away," *The Motley Fool*, 29 July 2017. Retrieved from www.fool.com/retirement/2017/07/29/9-baby-boomer-statistics-that-will-blow-you-away.aspx

The family members of seniors face special challenges.

Chapter Goal

The goal of this chapter is to address some concerns that the family members of seniors may run into. Make sure to go over these questions with your senior and your advisory team.

Hopefully, through an open conversation, you can discover any hidden plan disruptors and move towards a great outcome for your family.

Finalizing Your Plan

Are the last years of your senior family member's life going to be enjoyable for everyone or a great source of conflict?

Obviously, if a family member gets very sick or is in a lot of pain, things will not be enjoyable. However, what if your senior just starts slowing down a little but still has most of their mental faculties? What kind of plan are you going to put into place for your senior?

Family Impact

According to Rich Johnson at the Urban Institute, about 10% of Americans over the age of 65 have long-term care insurance.[21]

How are the other 90% of seniors going to pay for senior housing, and what kind of an impact will that have on their families?

Case Study

A young man sold his mom's house and moved her into an assisted living facility. The mom lived there for four years until her money ran out. She did not qualify for Medicaid nursing care, so he built a small house in the back of his primary residence, and he and his wife took turns taking care of his mom.

There is a special place in heaven for people who take care of their parents or grandparents. It can definitely be a blessing and a burden at the same time. The word that comes to mind in this situation is "sacrifice."

---

[21] Source: Gleckman, H. "Who Owns Long-Term Care Insurance?" *Forbes*, 18 August 2016, www.forbes.com/sites/howardgleckman/ 2016/08/18/who-owns-long-term-care insurance/#121f9d6f 2f05

Personal Experience

Max and his mom took turns caring for his grandmother. He said that it really did not feel like a burden because his grandmother was so nice to them and was pretty independent until the last few years.

The gradual transition did not seem like much of a burden because they had a really strong relationship in place before she needed a lot of assistance. As the years progressed, especially after she turned 80, she increasingly needed more and more help.

For more info, reach out to us at: www.cabinvestments.com, 708-316-0545, or mikeandmarisa@theseniorhousingbook.com.

Planning Help

If your relationship with your senior family member is strained or their condition gets worse quickly, this transition can be more difficult. If you are in a situation where you have to start caring for a senior family member, start by talking to all the family members and come up with a plan focusing on who will contribute financially or physically to the care.

Even if no one wants to help, it is better to know that from the beginning than to think one thing and find out something else. The best thing to do is to come up with a plan and work it out together.

If your senior needs more advanced help, who in your family is the best candidate to assist in this area? Who can you bring in?

Max's mom was a nurse, so when she was not working at the hospital, she was a natural fit as his grandmother's medical advisor.

Final Questions to Consider

Below are struggles that family members of seniors face and some recommendations on how to handle them. The questions in this and previous chapters are not a replacement for consulting professional counselors, advisors, and attorneys. They are a great starting point for getting some concerns out in the open so that you can come up with a plan to resolve them.

The questions, concerns, and challenges listed below have been sent in by our senior customer family members. We hope that these concerns and recommendations give your family clarity.

Family Member Challenges

Lack of Appreciation from Seniors Being Taken Care of by Family Members

Think back to when you were kids and your parents spent two hours preparing dinner. They would spend time slaving away on a gourmet meal, and how did you show your appreciation? "No thanks, I want something else!"

Maybe you were the exception. If you parent a large family, you hear that all the time. It is hard not to take it personally when you are not appreciated.

Are you going to be appreciated all the time when you are taking care of a senior family member? It depends. Even if your senior has a great disposition, when they are sick or in pain, it can be tough.

It is fine to tell your family member how you feel, but sometimes there is not much of a change. Be patient and find another family member or friend you can confide in.

Strained Relationships Before Care Began

If your relationship with your senior was strained before they got sick or needed your help, it is probably not going to get any better when more emotional, financial, and physical stress gets piled on top.

We highly recommend counseling. The more you can include a trained third-party advisor to help you, the better. Counseling can come from a trained family member, a church leader, or a private counselor. Most strained relationships did not get that way overnight, so do not expect the tension to dissipate immediately. However, you can start making progress today.

Caring for Seniors with Memory Issues

Your mood and energy are going to rub off on your senior. If you are positive and happy, it will encourage them and give you more patience. Speak to your senior in simple sentences and ask questions that involve 'yes' or 'no' answers. If your senior does not reply right away, be patient.

If you need your senior to do something that involves many steps, start with step 1 and do not talk about step 2 until step 1 is complete. If your senior gets mad at you, talk about something else or go for a walk. Maybe get something to eat. The change in scenery can help redirect the issue.

Sometimes, going through old photos can be a fun activity. Many seniors with memory issues cannot remember what you told them to do 30 minutes ago, but they can remember what was going on in a photo 30 years ago.[22]

Major Health Issues

According to a recent survey by the AARP Public Policy Institute and National Alliance for Caregiving, one in three people caring for someone at home hired paid help to assist them in the home.

If you are caring for a senior at home, start planning to get extra help, even if you do not need it right now. If your senior is over 55 years old and certified by the state as in need of nursing home-level care, see if the area you live in offers a PACE program, which is for people on Medicare or Medicaid. These programs cover in-home care, doctor care, and transportation. For more details, be sure to visit *https://www.medicare.gov/your-medicare-costs/get-help-paying-costs/pace*.[23]

---

[22] Source: "6 Best Ways to Stimulate Memories through Photos," *Alzheimers.net,* 6 October 2014. Retrieved from www.alzheimers.net/10-6-14-memories-photos

[23] Source: "PACE," *Medicare.* Retrieved from www.medicare.gov/your-medicare-costs/get-help-paying-costs/pace

Financial Issues

Hopefully, you got this book early in the process, so you now understand the enormous costs involved in senior care, and you can start working backwards to figure out what you are going to do.

Lack of communication contributes greatly to the stress factor. Many of the families we work with do not talk about money until they have to. Look into local programs for seniors offered by religious institutions and not-for-profit organizations like United Way.[24]

One Sibling Doing All the Work or Blocking Other People from Seeing the Senior

The sooner you start mapping out the role and contribution of everyone on the advisory team, the sooner you will get clarity on what the next steps are. If you are the sibling doing all the work in regard to taking care of your senior, let the other family members know that you need their help and ask them what they are willing or able to do. Do not assume anything.

[24] Source: "Aging," *United Way Worldwide*. Retrieved from www.unitedway.org/our-impact/featured-programs/aging

169

If there is a gatekeeper involved blocking you out, attempt to visit and help out. If that does not work, you can still send your senior letters and emails, letting them know you care about them.

Taking Care of Senior Parents while Still Taking Care of Children at Home

Will you be able to financially support your family and your parents at the same time? If not, who can you involve to help?

Is there physically enough room in your house for your family and your parents to live? Do you have the option of moving to a larger home or adding on to your existing home?

How will your senior parents integrate with your children? What will you do if there are disagreements?

How will you manage your time so that you can be with your spouse, children, and parents and still have time by yourself? How will you modify your schedule?

Feeling Guilty for Putting Your Parents in Senior Living Facilities

What is best for your senior?

Are you doing everything you can to make sure they will be in the best facility possible?

How can you still be involved with your senior and make them feel loved while they are living in a senior housing facility?

Each Adult Child Sibling Sees the Senior's Needs Differently

Who is the primary decision maker for the senior? Does everyone know who they are?

Are all the adult children part of the planning process? Have you included the concerns of all the adult children before you started putting your plan together?

The Senior Does Not Want to Admit That They Need Help

Have you explained your concerns to your senior? Have other children and family members expressed their concerns for their senior?

Are your concerns being presented as being bossy or caring?

Have you asked your senior why they do not feel the same way you do?

Is your senior still of sound mind? If not, have you contacted your attorney to investigate the guardianship process?

How to Pay for Senior Care

Are all family members involved in contributing to senior costs?

Is one family member the main decision maker for financial matters?

Have you consulted with your financial advisor for advice?

Have you contacted local churches and non-profits regarding free or reduced services for seniors?

Does your senior qualify for government or veteran benefits?

Caring for Both Parents at Once

Do you have enough financial, emotional, and physical strength to take care of both parents?

What are the different needs of each parent?

Can another family member move in or stop by regularly to help you take care of both parents?

In Closing

We hope that you have received a great deal of value from this book. Even one tip can make a huge difference in the outcomes for your senior. God bless you and your family during your senior housing journey. We will keep you all in our prayers.

For more info, reach out to us at: www.cabinvestments.com, 708-316-0545, or mikeandmarisa@theseniorhousingbook.com.

About Us
Mike Fisher & Marisa Rohrer

Mike and Marisa are passionate about their work with seniors in their community—helping them with the difficult decisions transition often brings, and improving their quality of life—but they are equally as passionate about family and raising their children in the ways of working hard and smart, being present, and solving problems.

They believe in strength of character being at the core of everything they do and strive to raise strong, independent, compassionate children, who live by the core values of living fully, loving openly, and making a difference to the world and the lives they touch, in everything they do.

At the cornerstone of their values is honesty, and Mike and Marisa believe that it is the foundation of building a strong character and living life admirably. They subscribe to the positive influence of surrounding themselves with people that lift and build their characters and challenge them to be better every day.

Max Keller

Max knows how to teach and create success. Max went from being a full-time high school Math Teacher to creating multiple successful real estate and marketing businesses. He has published multiple books and currently licenses his lead generation systems to real estate professionals all over the country.

Max loves the opportunity to teach, inspire, and share real-world applications that can transform the lives of business owners.

A few of his current roles are consultant, teacher, author, speaker, and expert panelist. He has flipped over 100 houses and is on a mission to help real estate professionals have customers chasing them.

Book Max to speak at your event at:

www.maxnkeller.com

Friend Max on Facebook:

www.facebook.com/Max.N.Keller

References

"14 Important Reverse Mortgage Facts," *New Retirement*, 12 January 2016. Retrieved from www.newretirement.com/ retirement/14-important-reverse-mortgage-facts/

"6 Best Ways to Stimulate Memories through Photos," *Alzheimers.net,* 6 October 2014. Retrieved from www.alzheimers.net/10-6-14-memories-photos/

"Aging & Health A to Z," *Health in Aging*. Retrieved from www.healthinaging.org/aging-and-health-a-toz/topic:nursin g-homes/

"Aging," *United Way Worldwide*. Retrieved from www.unitedway.org/our-impact/featured-programs/aging

Bernal, N. "Skilled Nursing Care: Fact vs. Myth," *Care Conversations*, 29 October 2014. Retrieved from careconversations.org/skilled-nursing-care-fact-vs-myth

"CCRC vs Rental Retirement Community | MyLifeSite Blog," *MyLifeSite*, 2 July 2018. Retrieved from www.mylifesite. net/blog/post/ccrc-vs-rental-retirement-community-what-are-the-differences/

"Cost of Care," The 2018 Cost of Care Report, *Genworth*. Retrieved from www.genworth.com/aging-and-you/ finances/cost-of-care.html

Frankel, M. "9 Baby-Boomer Statistics That Will Blow You Away," *The Motley Fool*, 29 July 2017. Retrieved from www.fool.com/retirement/2017/07/29/9-baby-boomer-statistics-that-will-blow-you-away.aspx

Fried, C. "Continuing Care Retirement Community: Can You Afford It?" *Time*, 22 December 2016. Retrieved from time.com/money/4579934/continuing-care-retirement-communities-cost/

"From Family Caregiving to Retirement Communities," *AARP*. Retrieved from www.aarp.org/caregiving/basics/info-2017/continuing-care-retirement-communities.html

Gleckman, H. "Who Owns Long-Term Care Insurance?" *Forbes*, 18 August 2016, www.forbes.com/sites/howardgleckman/2016/08/18/who-owns-long-term-care insurance/#121f9d6f 2f05

"Independent Living Community Price Ranges and Costs," *Brookdale Senior Living Solutions*. Retrieved from www.brookdale.com/en/where-to-begin/financial-considerations/independent-living-price-range.html

McKim, J. "More Seniors Are Taking Loans against Their Homes – And It's Costing Them," *The Washington Post*, 25 August 2017. Retrieved from www.washingtonpost.com/business/ economy/more-seniors-are-taking-loans-against-their-homes--and-its-costing-them/2017/08/25/5f154072-883a-11e7-961d-2f373b3977ee_story.html?utm_term=.831aa69 a5b55

"Medicare Supplemental Insurance Benefits for Assisted Living & Long-Term Care," *Medicare Supplemental Insurance (Medigap) Benefits for Long-Term Care*. Retrieved from www.payingforseniorcare.com/longtermcare/resources/medigap.html

"National Center for Health Statistics," *Centers for Disease Control and Prevention*, 3 May 2017. Retrieved from www.cdc.gov/nchs/fastats/life-expectancy.html

"Nursing Facilities," *Medicaid.gov*. Retrieved from www.medicaid.gov/medicaid/ltss/institutional/nursing/index.html

"PACE," *Medicare*. Retrieved from www.medicare.gov/your-medicare-costs/get-help-paying-costs/pace

"Residential Care, Such as Assisted Living, Memory Care, & Nursing Homes for Persons with Dementia," *Dementia Care Central*, 19 September 2018. Retrieved from www.dementiacarecentral.com/memory-care-vs-assisted-living/

"So I'll Probably Need Long-Term Care, But for How Long? *MyLifeSite*, 28 June 2018. Retrieved from www.mylifesite. net/blog/post/so-ill-probably-need-long-term-care-but-for-how-long/

Stark, E. "5 Facts You Should Know About Long-Term Care Insurance," *AARP*, 1 March 2018. Retrieved from www. aarp.org/caregiving/financial-legal/info-2018/long-term-care-insurance-fd.html

"What Is the Current Medicare Coverage for Long-Term Care?" *AARP*. Retrieved from www.aarp.org/health/medicare-qa-tool/current-long-term-nursing-home-coverage/

Made in the USA
Columbia, SC
22 February 2020